# UNLEA╎

## TH╌

# ARTIST

## WITHIN

### Breaking through Blocks and
### Restoring Creative Purpose

## ERIC MAISEL, PhD

ixia
PRESS

Mineola, New York

*Bibliographical Note*

*Unleashing the Artist Within: Breaking through Blocks and Restoring Creative Purpose*
is a new work, first published by Ixia Press in 2020.

*Library of Congress Cataloging-in-Publication Data*

Names: Maisel, Eric, 1947– author.
Title: Unleashing the artist within : breaking through blocks and restoring
creative purpose / Eric Maisel, PhD.
Description: Mineola, New York : Ixia Press, 2020. | Includes bibliographical
references and index.
Identifiers: LCCN 2019017265| ISBN 9780486831862 (alk. paper) | ISBN
0486831868 (alk. paper)
Subjects: LCSH: Creative ability. | Creation (Literary, artistic, etc.) | Artists—
Psychology.
Classification: LCC BF408 .M2327 2020 | DDC 153.3/5—dc23
LC record available at https://lccn.loc.gov/2019017265

Ixia Press
An imprint of Dover Publications, Inc.

Manufactured in the United States by LSC Communications
83186801
www.doverpublications.com/ixiapress

2 4 6 8 10 9 7 5 3 1

2019

# Contents

# Preface

Some years ago, I wrote a book called *Coaching the Artist Within*, in which I presented a dozen lessons of interest to creatives along with vignettes from my creativity coaching practice. This book, *Unleashing the Artist Within*, is a sequel to that book.

Many of the subjects presented here—I'm thinking particularly of tolerating the creative process, cracking through everyday resistance, healing from trauma, managing the daily grind, and completing creative projects and getting them out the door—deserve book-length treatments. There is a lot to say about these challenges! I hope that the discussions in this book, while not comprehensive, nevertheless help you.

I have been toiling away as a self-directing, self-employed creative for many years. It was fifty years ago that I started writing my first novel, a picaresque of my Army days in Korea, and thirty years ago that I started working with creative and performing artists, first as a therapist and then as a creativity coach. I recently did an interview and discovered—not to my chagrin but to my amusement—that I was grouped among the "elders" of the creativity community. So I guess I am officially an elder.

I've seen a lot during that time, firsthand and also through the eyes of the creativity coaches I train, the clients I work with, and the folks who attend my classes and workshops. The headline is that **I have never met one creative—not a single one—who had it easy.** Yes, a portion of that hardness was regularly self-created and self-imposed, for instance, because of unacknowledged performance anxiety, a stubborn resistance to dealing with the realities of the marketplace, or an unwillingness to maintain a regular creativity practice. But that it was self-created and self-imposed didn't make the hardness any less painful. I would say that it is axiomatic that every smart, sensitive, creative person is having a rough go of it.

The why of that I've discussed in about thirty books, this one included. That's a lot of books, a lot of challenges, and a lot of advice! The good news is you have an opportunity every day to choose an authentic life. I hope that the lessons contained in this book make your journey as a committed meaning-maker a little bit easier.

# Unleashing
## the
# Artist
## Within

# Chapter 1

## EMBRACING THE REALITIES OF PROCESS

The creative process is harder to tolerate and therefore harder to embrace than most people—the majority of creatives included—imagine, for a variety of reasons.

- Only a percentage of the work that we do turns out well. And only a percentage of that percentage is really excellent. This means that we have many "failed" efforts to endure, including countless mediocre works that may pass muster in the world but that don't thrill us much, internally count for much, or do such good a job of keeping the meaningfulness of creating afloat.

- The creative process involves making one choice after another. (For instance, "Should I send my character here or should I send him there?") and the activity of choosing provokes anxiety.

Just about every decision we make—say about buying this car or that car, changing our day job or staying put, accepting this not-very-fair gallery contract or rejecting it—produces anxiety, and the creative process is nothing but and exactly an endless series of choices. Given all that choosing—and given that, as a rule, we do not really love the experience of choosing—it's easy to see why you might not want to turn to your novel or your symphony as soon as you wake up.

■  The creative process involves going into the unknown, which can prove scary, especially if where we are going is into the recesses of our own psyche or to the place of reexperiencing trauma. Say that you are certain that you want to set a play during the Holocaust, but do you really want to spend hour after hour writing about Nazi torturers and their victims? Do you really want to be in that interrogation room? Your play may demand that you go there, but how likely is it that you actually will go there or be able to tolerate the experience once you are there?

■ The task we are setting ourselves—unraveling this scientific knot, creating that full-scale opera—may be beyond our intellectual or technical capabilities or may require information and understanding that we don't currently possess. Each individual's creative process is constrained by what he or she knows or can know.

■ The thing called "inspiration," which is one of the great joys of process and without which our work would prove lifeless, comes only periodically and can't be produced on demand. We must show up for what may prove days, weeks, months, and even years of slogging along with our creative project before a single brilliant ray of sunshine enlivens it and illuminates what we're doing. That is an idea that is very hard to tolerate—and even harder to tolerate as a reality.

The above is a fraction of the longer list of reasons why tolerating the creative process can prove so daunting and why fully embracing the realities of process can elude us. Most creatives do not grasp the extent to which this demanding process is itself stymieing them. They chalk up the fact that their novel remains unfinished to personal weakness or to their unfortunate circumstances and do not credit the reality of process as the real culprit.

The creative process can feel so daunting for a variety of reasons: not everything creatives attempt will turn out beautifully, many efforts will turn out ordinary, and a significant number will prove flat-out not very good. A composer writes a hit Broadway musical, and the next one is abysmal. No one can believe it's the same person! A novelist pens a brilliant first novel, and the second one is unreadable. What a disappointment! A physicist comes *thisclose* to a breakthrough but doesn't break through, rendering his several years of work "worthless." How demoralizing! These are everyday occurrences in the lives of creatives and the rule rather than the exception. How to stay calm in the face of this?

What to do? Of course, you must do everything required to make the work good, including getting quiet, showing up, honestly appraising, and all the rest. But in addition to all that, you must maturely accept the reality of missteps, mistakes, messes, lost weeks (and even lost years), and unhappy outcomes. To help with this effort, do the following: hang a still life painting of a bowl of apricots on a wall in the room that is your mind. Have that bowl be filled with gorgeous, ripe apricots and also with mottled, discolored, overripe apricots. The reason for installing this painting and the lesson from this painting? That you must calmly and gracefully take the bad with the good.

Romantic painters not understanding the point of this lesson would make sure to paint only gorgeous apricots. Likewise, superrealist painters in preparing their still life would pick only the best apricots to include, unless they were intending to make a point about decay. Virtually no painters, past or present, would fill their bowl with beautiful *and* rotten apricots. That goes against our ingrained ideas about beauty and about what a painting is "supposed to do." The painting you hang in the room that is your mind, however, is not being hung there for its beauty.

It is being hung there to remind you about the reality of process. It is being hung there to remind you that you must take the bad with the good as you create. It is being hung there to remind you to be your most mature self, the "you" who understands that you are bound to produce work all along the spectrum from lousy to brilliant and back again. This mature acceptance, once you really accept it, is deeply calming.

Among his hundreds of cantatas, Bach's most famous cantata is number 140. His top ten would likely be composed of numbers 4, 12, 51, 67, 80, 82, 131, 140, 143, and 170. What about the other hundreds? Are some merely workmanlike and unmemorable? Yes. Are others not very interesting at all? Yes. Was Bach obliged to live with that reality? Yes. As must you. Yes, you might completely by accident produce a brilliant first thing and then never try again and so ensure your success rate at 100 percent. But is that a way to live a life? Or, rather, is that the perfect way to avoid living?

Hang a painting of a bowl of apricots filled with lovely ripe apricots and quite unlovely overripe apricots in a prominent place on one of the walls in the room that is your mind. It is not there to reprimand you, chastise you, or discourage you. Rather, it is there to remind you about the reality of process, a reality that no human being can escape or evade. Every once in a while, when your creative or intellectual work is going poorly or when you've created something that fails to meet your standards, stand in front of that painting, sigh, and murmur, "Process."

Honoring and embracing the realities of process and calmly living with those realities are choices you get to make. The word to underline in that sentence? *Calmly*. Anxiety is a natural feature of the human condition and a much larger feature than most people realize. A great deal of what we do in life we do in order to reduce our experience of anxiety or to avoid the experience of anxiety. Because life can feel dangerous in all sorts of ways—from walking down a dark alley to giving a two-minute talk at work—and because anxiety is a feature of our warning system that alerts us to danger, anxiety is a prominent feature of daily life.

It also is a very prominent feature of the creative process. When I ask you to embrace the realities of the creative process, I also am asking you to embrace the reality of anxiety as a prominent feature of that process. You do not want to avoid creating just because creating or the prospect of creating is making you anxious. No, you want to manage that anxiety, or if it can't quite be managed beautifully, then create while anxious. What you don't want to get in the habit of doing is avoiding the creative encounter because of your anxious feelings. You know that you don't want that to be your way of dealing with the everyday, ordinary anxiety that attaches to process.

*Creativity* is the word we use for our desire to make use of our inner resources; employ our imagination; knit together our thoughts and our feelings into beautiful things like songs, quilts, or novels; and feel like the hero of our own story. It is the way that we manifest our potential, make use of our intelligence, and embrace what we love. When we create, we feel whole, useful, and devoted. You don't want your experience of anxiety to prevent you from having all that. The anxiety that is such a prominent feature of human nature can and does prevent us from creating. Now is the time to come to a deep acceptance of that truth.

Why do we get so anxious around creating? There are many reasons. We get anxious because we fear we may fail, because we fear we may disappoint ourselves, because the work can be extremely hard, because the marketplace may criticize us and reject us. We want to create because that is a wonderful thing to do, but we also don't want to create so as to spare ourselves all that anxiety. That is the profound dilemma that confronts and afflicts countless smart, sensitive, creative souls. And, as a result, most creatives spend a lot of time defensively avoiding creating.

Our quite human defensiveness is one of the primary ways that we try to avoid experiencing anxiety. We deny what we're experiencing; try to rationalize away what we're experiencing; misname what we're experiencing as sickness, weakness, or confusion; get angry at our mate so as to have something else to focus on. We are very tricky creatures in this regard. It would be good if we did a much better job of frankly accepting that we are feeling anxious and then managing those feelings. That would give us a much better shot at tolerating the anxieties that come with the creative process. But most people are more inclined to react defensively than forthrightly when it comes to anxiety.

What should creatives do instead of fleeing the encounter or managing their anxiety in ineffective or unhealthy ways (say, by using alcohol to calm their nerves)? They should:

- Acknowledge and accept that anxiety is a regular feature of the process.
- Assert that they won't allow anxiety to derail them or silence them.
- Demand of themselves that they practice and learn effective anxiety management skills.

It is too big a shame not to create if creating is what you long to do. The thing to do instead is to become an anxiety expert and get on with your creating. What can help in addition to mastering anxiety management skills? Create an anxiety vow in which you pledge not to let anxiety silence you. Your vow might sound something like this: "I will create, even if creating provokes anxiety in me. When it does provoke anxiety, I will manage it through the use of the anxiety management skills I am learning and practicing." Or you might prefer the shorter, crisper "Bring it on!"

Since both creating and not creating produce anxiety, you might as well embrace the fact that anxiety will accompany you on your journey as a creative person. Just embracing that reality will release a lot of the ambient anxiety that you feel. Return to your current project right now with a new willingness to accept the reality of anxiety. Since anxiety accompanies both states—both creating and not creating— isn't it the case that you might as well choose creating?

## Draft after Draft

One spring I found myself in London presenting at the First World Congress for Existential Therapy. Having grown up at the height of French existentialism, a fan of Sartre and Camus, and a firm believer in the basic ideas of existential- ism (about freedom, personal responsibility, authenticity, and absurdity), I'm curious to see where existentialism has traveled over the decades.

The conference turns out not to be quite to my taste, but London definitely is. London is one of my favorite places. I first came to London in 1974 by way of two months in Iceland, where it had been bitterly cold, which helped explain why I was wearing a pink parka in the middle of spring. London didn't mind my odd attire. Why would it? As a cosmopolitan stop on the international bohemian highway, London was up for such sights.

That spring I roomed for a few months with a democrat and an aristocrat in a flat off the Finchley Road. The democrat was friendly and the aristocrat snooty. I had my own room and worked on my second novel, with sun pouring in through large windows. The democrat invited me to concerts: he accompanied lieder singers on the piano. The aristocrat brought home a different woman each night, for whom he cooked. He seduced his dates with beef bourguignonne and filled the flat with French aromas. In the middle of the night, I would sneak into the kitchen and eat their leftovers.

One free afternoon during my current sojourn in London I meet with a new client at the Freemasons Arms, a pub off Hampstead Heath. My new client is a tall, thin University of London professor of history who has never finished writing a single book he's begun.

We sit in the back with our pints. It is a glorious spring day, and the garden is full. John begins.

"I write drafts," he says.

"Drafts are good," I reply, smiling.

"If they lead to finished books. For me, they don't."

I wait.

"Let me tell you a little bit about myself," he commences. "I grew up with mentally ill parents. After years of therapy, I think I've come to identify a kind of demon who comes into my consciousness and does not want me to be productive or successful. That demon was born in childhood. It somehow has to do with safety. It did not feel safe living with my parents, plus they told us that the world wasn't a safe place. They filled our lives with continual anxiety and catastrophizing."

I nod and wait.

"Here's how that all plays out now. My creativity starts to flow and then anxiety floods in. I tear up the work, I tear myself down, and I abandon the project as no good. I'm also flooded with feelings of intense dread all the time, especially at night. And during the day, I'm always finding ways of avoiding entering my writing space." He takes a sip. "That's easy enough, as I have classes to teach, committee meetings, a bit of a commute, and all the rest. It's supremely easy to avoid my study. I can't tell you what a shame that is, because my study is so lovely." He laughs briefly. "I wanted to say 'lovely and inviting,' but it doesn't invite me."

"You've started many books?"

"Many."

"All on sort of the same subject?"

"Yes. The year 1946 in England, France, and Germany. Something about that postwar year has always intrigued me. But the landscape is vast—larger than vast. One small event in one of those countries could be worth a book. I get overwhelmed."

I nod. "So the whole tableau feels impossible to capture, but any piece of it feels too small to bother with?"

"That's accurate. Plus, my peers keep writing about that time period, as it seems to have gotten under the skin of countless European historians—rather like your Civil War still hypnotizes so many of your historians. And so every time I hear one of my peers talk about their latest book or article or watch them perform beautifully at a conference where they share their ideas, that further contributes to my inner difficulties. Those experiences map on to an already existing damaged force field within, a dark, trancelike inner blackness or darkness."

We sit quietly.

"These demons have made it harder for me to keep meaning afloat in my life, they've made it harder for me to keep despair at bay, they've made it harder for me to live my life purposes, and they've contributed to my anxiety and depression diagnoses. It's all of a piece. I've come a certain distance in all this and I can function, but I'm still searching for answers and wanting to finish a damned book. So here I am."

We are getting near to needing another pint.

"I think that the bottom line for me is that the demon won't budge, because it is about core safety," John says quietly. "Therefore, I must celebrate lesser forms of creativity where the emotional stakes and pressures are low. An article, maybe, though articles aren't easy either! I haven't found ways to conquer the demons of darkness but I do intend to continue to work on this block through some kind of inner demon work. I haven't quite given up. Not quite."

"What project would you like to get completed?" I wonder out loud.

He shakes his head. "I can't get close to thinking about that."

"Talking about it now makes you anxious?"

"Completely!"

"Okay. Let's try the following. I'd like you to picture a snow globe. You know what I mean?"

"Yes. Bizarrely enough, I collect them."

"Great! Let's put a scene in ours. How about the South Bank and the London Eye?"

"All right," he consents. "Should I include the Tate Modern? And all the bridges? And the motor launches heading toward Greenwich?"

This is how anxiety manifests. This manifestation is sometimes incorrectly called perfectionism, the need in John's case to create the perfect scene in his imagined snow globe. But "getting it perfect" has nothing to do with it.

"Not to worry." I laugh. "Just shut your eyes. Picture that snow globe. Now shake it up. A great snowstorm has hit London," I say, smiling. "Got that picture?"

"I do." He shakes his head. "A rare occurrence."

"But not in snow globes."

"Indeed."

We both smile.

"Now, calmly watch the snow settle," I continue. "That great storm is getting lighter and lighter. It's hardly a flurry. As the snow settles, let your nerves settle. When the snow has settled, let's try my question again."

He sits with his eyes shut. After a few more moments, he nods, his eyes still closed.

"All right," I say. "What book would you like to get written?"

He sighs heavily. "One about how Nazi collaborators were treated in those three countries in that first postwar year."

"That's very clear. What's the intellectual challenge associated with that?"

He opens his eyes. "Good question." He thinks for a bit. "That it's too vast a subject. Just how they were treated in one corner of the Alsace would require a trilogy."

"Let's deal with that," I continue. "How can you make this a manageable book, one that on the one hand can get done and that on the other hand doesn't get too reduced in scope as to bore you or feel trivial?"

That got John thinking. Suddenly, he shakes his head. "I've known the answer all along. It's to treat one specific collaborator in each country and let him or her stand for the dynamics of that period. I even know exactly who they will be. I've got tons of research notes on three superinteresting figures: one a Londoner, one in rural France, and one in Berlin. And I love the diversity of their outcomes: one commits suicide, one is executed, and one makes it all the way back to prominence. It's a wonderful playing out of those dynamics!"

The right question can work wonders, as can the right answer. We both knew that John had landed on exactly the right answer. That amounted to a superb beginning . . . but only a beginning.

"Great!" I exclaim. "Now you know exactly what you are doing. That will make the process much easier . . . but only so much easier. You still have to tolerate the reality of what it takes to write a book."

"I know. I don't know if I can."

"Of course. That remains to be seen. But understanding your book is an invaluable first step. Now, let's see what we have to think about next."

"Getting me into my study."

"No." I smile. "I think that now that you know what your book is about, you'll actually want to enter your study. The question is, will you be able to stay put?"

"And will I?" John laughs.

Then he falls quiet. I know that John is picturing being in his study, working on this book. He is picturing masses of notes, intolerable messes, unbearable silences, parts that won't fit, and all the rest. He shakes his head. It's clear that a powerful doubt that he can pull this immense task off has arisen.

"Your demons?" I inquire.

"Yes. They are really coming out in full force."

"Say no to them. Say, 'No, not this time.'"

John surprises me by exclaiming, "No! Not this time!" A number of our neighboring drinkers turn to stare. "An exorcism," John says to a woman nearest him on his right. She nods and smiles. This being London, she has no problem with pub exorcisms.

John and I work together for the next three years, chatting via Skype once a month. There are many downs but also enough ups that John finishes a draft of his book, deals with its several revisions, sends it on its journey into the world of academic presses, tolerates the criticisms and rejections his manuscript initially receives, enjoys that moment that it is accepted for publication, and learns that his editor has many requests before she sees it as suitable for publication. I keep reminding him, "This is the process." And at some point, he begins to laughingly beat me to the punch and becomes the first to announce, "I know: this is the process!"

The book actually makes a small splash, which few books put out by academic presses do. This doesn't quite make John happy, as happiness is an elusive commodity in the lives of sentient beings. But it does make John smile. Yes, that smile may have been tinged with a little irony, but it is nevertheless a bit warming on one of those gloomy London days.

# Chapter 2

## BREAKING THROUGH EVERYDAY RESISTANCE

Most creatives are confronted every day by a thin veneer of resistance that stands between them and their creative work. As thin as this everyday veneer of resistance is, it is real and it is surprisingly hard to crack. This resistance, arising for a variety of reasons—a little bit of ambient anxiety, a little bit of fear of ruining the piece, a little worry about not knowing where to go next, a little doubt that the project is really viable or valuable, a little shame at procrastinating so long and not getting it done sooner—is as thin as the thinnest sheet of ice . . . but just as solid.

There are many obstacles to unlocking your creative potential and unleashing the artist within. One is simply not having enough time or taking enough time to be an artist. Squeezing in fifteen minutes here and fifteen minutes there is not a path to unlocking potential. You need time to dream the work, time to create the work, time to appraise the work, time for ideas to percolate, time to experiment, and time to fully inhabit your artist identity. A second is maintaining too noisy a mind, one that is constantly filled with busy thoughts about errands, worries, regrets, unwashed laundry, and a hundred other things. It is hard for a mind this busy to dream up grand ideas or to fully function in the service of art-making. A third is managing the anxiety that comes with the creative process and the creative life. If, because you are anxious, you want to flee your creative work, that isn't a situation very conducive to unlocking potential.

There are many other challenges as well: not taking yourself seriously enough, not really engaging your imagination, not healing early traumas and wounds, and more. These include all of the ones we're addressing in the book, from restoring meaning when it vanishes to speaking up and asking for what you need. All of these are at least somewhat familiar to you. What may be more unfamiliar is the idea that we are *at least a little resistant to getting to our creative work just about all the time*. This special difficulty sits alongside or on top of all of our other difficulties and can put creating completely out of reach.

This everyday resistance causes would-be artists to make up false tales about what creativity is, especially the tale that it is something that you must wait for, as in "I need to be inspired in order to create." An artist had better not wait to be inspired before beginning to work, because inspiration typically only comes to artists who are willing to work when *not* inspired. If you are not cracking through everyday resistance in an everyday way, it is highly unlikely that inspiration will have any way to visit.

Tchaikovsky put it this way: "I'm inspired about every fifth day but I only get that fifth day if I show up the other four days." This is one of the great truths about the creative process and the creative life: that if you sit on your hands waiting for inspiration and do not deal with your everyday resistance to creating, you will likely be sitting there next month and next year. That thin veneer of resistance is not likely to thaw of its own accord. You must crack through it. How to crack through it?

1. **Create and maintain an art practice.** If you get in the habit of showing up every day to your art, come hell or high water, then you have completely solved the problem of a lack of motivation and everyday resistance on those uninspired days. Yes, you may and must skip

some days, as you have other life purposes, duties, and reasons for being, but don't skip too many. If you let three or four days pass, six months may vanish.

2. **Remember that work in the service of meaning may not feel meaningful.** Meaning is a certain sort of psychological experience that we crave. But to get that fleeting feeling of meaningfulness from the painting, novel, or sonata we're working on, we must work, even if the work is tedious, even if we doubt ourselves, even if the work is taxing. A week of drudgery may get you only a split second of meaning, but you wouldn't have gotten that split second otherwise. This is a headline point: **work in the service of meaning may not feel meaning-ful on any given day.** Do not say things to yourself like "My novel doesn't feel important to me." Maybe it doesn't *feel* very important to you today, but that doesn't mean that it *isn't* important. Instead say, "I matter, and my efforts matter." No phrase and no sentiment are more vital than that one!

3. **Cultivate some tactics for getting inspired.**
   What inspires you? Certain music? The works of
   a particular artist? Special quotations? For me, if
   I dip into the notebooks of Camus, I find myself
   drifting off to a place that promotes rich writing.
   What works for you? Make a list of "The Ways
   I Know to Get Inspired," keep that list handy,
   and make use of it when the dull days begin to
   mount up. Given that our everyday resistance
   to creating may confront us *every day*, you may
   want to get in the habit of doing something
   ceremonially motivating every single day.

4. **Hold "inspiration" as a reward and not
   a gift.** Mental models matter. If you hold the
   creative process one way, as something outside of you that you are searching for, waiting
   for, or aching for, you will let long stretches of
   time slip away. If you hold the creative process as more like cultivating a garden, where
   toil and mystery meet, then you will water
   and weed that garden in a regular way and
   amazing flowers will appear. Hold inspiration
   as something you earn, like salad from your
   own garden.

Remember how the creative process actually works: inspiration is real but it must be earned by paying attention to the work at hand, by being with the work, by not saying things like "I have no talent" or "I have no idea what I'm doing." Reprising the headline from chapter one, what you want to say instead is "Process." Let that rich, powerful, truthful word remind you that the creative process is exactly what it is: a pathway to wonderful, occasional inspiration for those who crack through their daily resistance.

The reality that inspiration is only an occasional guest means that not everything you do will feel inspired or look inspired. You may produce a few dull paintings for every lively one; so be it. You may spend a month unhappy that your creations look dull; so be it. There's a reason that every great artist's work has a varied impact on us: some of it is more successful and some of it is less successful; some of it is more inspired and some of it is less inspired. Every artist must live with that reality, you and me included.

You can see why cracking through everyday resistance is so difficult, as it has so many "causes." What is the word that we tend to use for our failure to crack through our everyday resistance to creating? *Procrastination*. Who doesn't procrastinate? It's a natural human tendency, given that the thing we need to do may be making us anxious, may feel too difficult to accomplish, may come with risks (like failure or exposure), or may involve us stretching in uncomfortable ways. Here we are again, coming up against our everyday resistance and blockage.

Say that you have an ambitious painting in mind. But you know that it will tax your drawing skills. Plus, it's a complicated composition. Plus, it will use up a lot of your expensive pigments. Plus, its subject matter is on the controversial side and may get you snide comments and other forms of pushback. Plus, it's time-consuming and you hate the idea of spending months on a project that may not pan out. Plus, you have a worry that the idea is silly. Plus, it feels unlikely to sell—who will want a painting as huge as the one you're contemplating? Plus . . .

Who wouldn't procrastinate, thinking all these half-paralyzing thoughts? Virtually anyone. So what can you do in common situations like this one? While you are working through these worries, your best course of action is to *procrastinate by being productive*. Maybe facing the painting in question is simply an impossibility at this moment. Then pick something useful to do from your, no doubt, long list of creative tasks or art career tasks and do one of them. Contact that gallery owner. Update your website. Work on that other painting. Be productive. That's the very best way to procrastinate!

These may prove to be among your most productive times. Oddly energized by not having to face the task that is making you anxious and aware that you are giving yourself the gift of attending to important items on your to-do list that you hadn't anticipated getting to, you may find yourself zipping through tasks that had themselves been sources of paralysis and procrastination. Updating your artist statement had been taking *forever*—now you get it done in a flash because it is experienced as ever so much easier work than facing that huge painting. How interesting!

Now you have this simple, effective, healthy approach to procrastination: you will *procrastinate by being productive*. This is a grand idea and one that has worked beautifully for me. I hope that you add it to your repertoire of excellent self-coaching skills. Indeed, you could choose this as your "cracking through everyday resistance" mantra: I procrastinate by being productive.

Mantras, ceremonies, and other tactics are quite necessary, since the problem of our everyday resistance to creating is both so common and insidious. To take one category of creatives, most writers find it inexplicably hard to do the thing that abstractly sounds relatively easy to do: write a little bit each day. What is the essence of the problem? Any given writer might write twenty novels in ten years' time: that's a mere two pages a day for those ten years. But who actually writes twenty novels from, say, the age of twenty-five to the age of thirty-five? Except for the occasional romance writer, no one. What's much more common is for a writer to write a draft of one novel and half a draft of another novel in those ten years—and feel terribly disappointed about her outcome.

A mere two pages a day. When we're lost in the trance of writing, that's no more than an hour of writing. An hour of writing a day, two pages of writing a day: isn't it amazing that it should turn out to be so hard to accomplish this simple-sounding daily work? This is further proof of how hard it is to crack through our everyday resistance to creating. This difficulty is made doubly hard because we aren't noticing it as resistance or labeling it as resistance. The following exercise can help massively in that regard.

Picture an egg. If you want to crack that egg because you are baking a cake, you tap it carefully on the side of a bowl or countertop, it breaks, and you drop the contents of the egg into the bowl of flour. There's nothing simpler. But if the egg is just sitting there and you are not baking a cake, its shell is going to feel formidable. There is something almost scary about cracking an egg for no good reason, something that makes us squeamish, like a violation of the egg, something very dramatic about breaking that hard shell and having the contents ooze out.

If we are baking a cake, we think nothing of cracking an egg. If we aren't baking a cake, that egg is something of a strange fortress with which we do not want to tamper. Cracking that egg for no good reason is almost beyond us, but cracking the egg for the sake of getting on with our cake is child's play. There is a big secret here. If you can get a good visceral sense of that hard shell protecting an egg and what it feels like to crack an egg open, you will suddenly better understand what our everyday resistance to creating feels like in the body.

To learn how to make use of this egg metaphor and this egg reality, I'd like you to put an egg, a bowl, and a spoon beside your computer, if you're a writer, and begin your daily writing session by cracking that egg into the bowl, egg and shell fragments all, and then turning directly to your work.

Experience that cracking of the egg as the cracking through of your resistance. Feel yourself exhale as you crack it, as if you have survived something dangerous. Proceed on to your writing, feeling safe that you are on the other side of the resistance. That is step one: crack an egg and write (or paint, compose, practice your instrument, and so on).

A second area of resistance is our unwillingness to stay put. We write some, hit a hard patch, and abandon our work for the day. I want you to change that dynamic and stay put longer. This week, I want you to create for hours, not minutes. You can do this, in part, by thinking of yourself as a day laborer and not as an artist. You are simply a worker, toiling in the fields of words, feelings, ideas, and the imagination. Nothing fussy; nothing flighty; nothing airy-fairy; just righteous hard work ahead of you.

Remember that you brought a spoon along with you to your creating space, along with that egg and bowl. Now you get to use that spoon. Whenever you stop because you have encountered a trouble spot or are experiencing a momentary resistance, take the spoon and calmly and patiently stir that messy egg-and-shell mixture in the bowl beside you. Just stir it and say something in a meditative way, as if you were chanting a mantra. You might say, "I don't mind messes." You might say, "I haven't worked enough yet." You might say, "I'm not leaving. I'm just stirring." Try out various phrases.

Your goal is to not leave your creating because you feel like leaving. You will only leave when you are done. When are you done? Not when your weak self says, "Enough!"

You will only leave when your warrior self says, "Very good. That was an honorable creative stint."

I'd love you to do the following three things every day this week:

1. Create, because you want and need to create.

2. Begin each session by cracking an egg.

3. Leave only when you are really done and no sooner.

When I train creativity coaches, I have them engage with this exercise. Here's the report from one coach-in-training, Beatriz:

"I've always liked eggs, not only as food, but as objects in themselves. They've got a very beautiful shape, texture, and weight, and I like the fact that they fit in one hand that becomes like a nest. I've photographed them, drawn them, and included them in my performative videos. For me, they are strong metaphors of birth, death, fragility, protection, transformation, mystery, and fertility. They always inspire me.

"I'm sitting right now in front of my computer with a bowl at my side, ready to fulfill Eric's assignment and crack an egg before I start to work. He wants it to be a metaphor for breaking through my resistances to creating, and I'm really happy to give the egg full power to help me do this task. I'm taking this homework very seriously because I believe in the power of rituals and I want to turn this act into one. Rituals are, for me, food for my right brain, direct messages to my subconscious, doorsteps for big changes.

"When I first read the assignment and I pictured myself cracking the egg for no useful purpose, I felt a contraction in my body. I could feel the fear. Why? Cracking an egg for no purpose is a violent act, and it is also a waste. I suddenly made the connection. Art is a waste. For many years, I've been feeling that art-making was not something really useful. I remembered my ethical conflicts about this subject when I volunteered to work one summer in London with homeless people. Twice a week we went to Hyde Park with a van and gave out hot soup and tea. The reality of this life had a big impact on me. It made me feel ashamed of studying art at that time.

"Art felt superfluous compared to the job I was doing. Art fulfilled expressive and aesthetic needs, but those needs were unimportant compared to the needs of food and shelter. An inner voice started to talk inside of me and said things like: 'You are selfish to worry about what to paint. Look at these people! They don't have what to eat! That is really a problem, not what color to use. What do you expect from your paintings? To sell them to somebody rich who will hang them on their wall? Don't you think there are better ways to spend that money than buying paintings?' The voice kept going and going, and it was so strong at times that I really considered giving up my career and becoming a volunteer in India or Africa.

"I realize that being useful to others gave me an immediate sense of worth that was really rewarding. It felt great in comparison to what art-making was giving me at that time: anxiety; fears; doubts; feelings of unworthiness, selfishness, and loneliness. As I write this paragraph, I clearly see that turning my career toward teaching and therapy was an understandable shift to pursue those feelings of worthiness that I think started that summer. I've also always feared becoming a narcissistic, egocentric artist whom nobody could love, while being a 'nice and generous teacher and therapist' seemed like something very lovable.

"I take a big breath, hold the egg in my hand, feel its weight, and throw it violently into the bowl. I think there is anger in my gesture. I was expecting a big splash and a big mess, and it didn't happen. The egg stays upright, and the white starts appearing at the bottom. I pick up the shell, and the yolk slides out intact, much to my surprise. The shell is also in one piece, smashed but holding together. I look with incredulity at how I've been able to crack an egg violently without making a mess. I smile. Maybe my resistance isn't that scary or messy after all? It seemed like an Everest mountain, impossible to climb for so many years, but I recognize and enjoy how accessible it seems now.

"Another summer memory comes to mind. Two years ago, a friend of mine lent me his house on the beach near Barcelona for ten days to work on my art again. It was the first time I gave myself this opportunity in years. The house was gorgeous, with wooden ceilings, tall walls, and big windows. The architect and my friend had really done a wonderful job designing the house, and I got very inspired. One day I was sitting at the table, editing my video, and I looked through the window and suddenly became overwhelmed by a feeling of complete happiness. Tears started to fall from my eyes. I was so fulfilled and felt such gratitude toward my friend for giving me the opportunity to create again in such a beautiful spot that I had to text him a thank-you message.

"At that moment, I became at peace with the pursuit of the aesthetic qualities of art-making. I understood that beauty is a high energy vibration and that I'm sensitive to it. When I'm in a beautiful place or in front of a beautiful work of art, I vibrate in that same energy, and that makes me happy and fulfilled. Art and beauty have value. Maybe they don't feed homeless people in Hyde Park, but they definitely feed my soul. I think I didn't realize until that moment that it wasn't only the contemplation of art and beauty that made me so happy, but to feel real fulfillment, creating art was a necessary part of that total experience.

"Art is not a superfluous activity, nor a selfish activity. Art is the activity that helps me create and give meaning to my life. And if I don't create, I become spiritually dead. It hurt to read those words today. I've been spiritually dead for a long time, searching for answers in thousands of therapies and theories, without realizing that my path, my language, my home, my power laid in creating art. There are no excuses, no running away anymore. I've cracked the egg, I've crossed the threshold, I've made the commitment.

"I intend to keep cracking eggs this whole week, not because it is useful or sensible, but because it helps me create meaning and makes me happy, it honors my life and feeds my soul, and it is my own intimate way to contact the sacred within me. I'm going to keep cracking eggs as I wish, sometimes gently, sometimes violently, sometimes happily, sometimes with sadness, sometimes in reality, and sometimes only in my mind, because I recognize the power of rituals and images and I know the symbol lives within me. I can access it whenever I want. I'm going to crack eggs and keep doing my thing. I just looked at the clock and four hours have passed. I haven't had to stir the egg once. I think I've been an impeccable warrior today and beautifully fulfilled my task."

It would be lovely if we didn't have to crack through everyday resistance, if that resistance weren't there at all. How much easier it would then be to get on with our art-making! But that everyday resistance is a signature reality in the lives of creatives and would-be creatives, and so it must be recognized and reckoned with. Think about this lesson carefully. Has a thin veneer of *something* long stood between you and your creative efforts? If so, isn't it time for you to find your way of cracking through it?

# Chapter 3

## GETTING HUNGRY

A lack of motivation, a lack of desire, and a lack of appetite can keep you from unleashing your creative potential. Many creatives announce that they want to create and claim to be interested in their own ideas, yet they seem to have no real appetite for their creative work and no real hunger to create. Where did their appetite go? Or was it never there?

Often there is an important but hard-to-define causal relationship between a need for control and a loss of appetite. For blocked creatives, it sounds like "You can't make me create." With whom are they engaged in stubborn battle? A parent? Themselves? The marketplace? The universe?

Would-be creatives are not sufficiently hungry when it comes to their creating. They literally have no appetite for their own creative efforts. Is it that their efforts to maintain a grip on ordinary life suppress their creative appetite to such an extent that they end up with no real chance? Whatever the exact relationship between stubborn control and creative anorexia may be, if you are among those without a real appetite for creating, you will need to whet your own appetite.

Many would-be creative people find themselves in this odd situation, firm but not proud in their conviction that there is nothing in life that genuinely interests them or that can genuinely interest them. They claim that they would dearly love it if something did passionately interest them, and yet their claim sounds a little hollow. Is it really the case that a person in decent health and in decent spirits wouldn't find ice cream, pizza, barbecued ribs, or *something* tasty? Or is it rather that they are in poor existential spirits and down on life in some special way, such that their appetite has been suppressed and even ruined?

Whatever the precise reasons for this malaise, countless smart, sensitive, creative people find themselves wasting away, in love with nothing, and convinced that likely at first glance, but certainly at second glance, all pursuits are bound to turn empty.

Nothing seems able to provoke the psychological experience of meaning in them. They read a novel: that was okay; now what? They plant roses: that was okay; now what?

They learn carpentry: they make a few objects; now what? They take a class: that was interesting enough; now what? They start a business: the stress outweighs the rewards; on to the next thing. They do things mildly, pleasantly, and somehow to no avail.

People who stand as hobbyists-in-life and who are bereft of drive, meaning, and motivation are bound to despair. Yet there is an odd stubbornness to their plight, as if they are determined not to give up their worldview even if another worldview might come with meaning and might motivate them. Just as addicts fiercely hold on to their addictions and will only pay lip service—or no service at all—to the idea of recovery and the rewards of a life without their cigarettes, cocaine, or alcohol, many smart, sensitive, creative people become attached to both a life empty of meaning and to an addiction—the addiction soothing the pain produced by their stubborn refusal to take a genuine stab at making meaning.

Here's how Sandra, a client of mine, described her situation:

"At forty-nine, I find that I have not been able to sustain interest in anything really. Art in the broadest sense is the closest thing. I like it all, but nothing really sticks. There's nothing that I'm specifically passionate about. But I wish there was. I can't help but feel that if I concentrate on one activity, I will be missing out on another. Am I greedy? Do I have the passion but not the focus? I envy artists who can explore their subjects in-depth over time. It feels like I will live my whole life trying to decide what I want to be when I grow up."

No doubt each hunger artist became a hunger artist in their own way. There is no single path to a lifetime of acute meaninglessness. There are so many ways to kill off meaning: by not caring, by not committing, by not finding the courage, by not choosing, by not besting demons, by not standing up, by not declaring that life is worth the candle. One answer? Make sure that there is a place in the room—a certain chair, a certain corner, a certain nook—where the instant you arrive, you feel ravenous. In this way, you'll cultivate your appetite, not for peanuts, Scotch, or gadgets, but for meaning and life purpose. Make sure that such a place exists and visit it regularly!

Would-be creatives never make this connection. They do not quite see that they are without any particular appetite for the creative tasks they claim they want to pursue. In my work with clients, I've had countless head-shaking variations on the following conversation:

"I love painting," my new client will say.

"Great! It's good to have loves."

"But I never paint."

"Ah. Why is that?"

"Too busy."

"Oh. You never get a Saturday or Sunday off?"

"Oh, sure. I get every Saturday and Sunday off from my day job. But there's always so much to do."

"You mean, like the laundry? That sort of thing?"

"Exactly."

"But even so, you could get in a couple of hours of painting on a Saturday, even with all those other things to do. Couldn't you?"

"I suppose."

"Then why not get in a couple of hours of painting this Saturday?"

"Well, my wife doesn't like me hiding out on the weekends just painting."

"She would miss you for an hour or two on a Saturday morning?"

"Maybe. I don't know."

"So that might be worth a try?"

"Maybe."

"You say you love painting?"

"Yes!"

"I don't hear much love of painting in what you're saying."

"I do love painting! It's just that I need to get away for a week on a painting retreat and immerse myself in painting! That's what I need."

"And you've planned such a trip?"

"No."

"Why not?"

"Because the family really wants to go to Disney World. We only have money for one vacation, and it has to be Disney World."

"Oh."

It isn't precisely that this person and the others like him are making excuses. Of course, they *are* making excuses. But their challenge isn't to "stop making excuses." It's to excavate to the place where the reasons for their loss of appetite can be fathomed. That may be a very deep, very dark, very painful place—a place known as despair.

Hunger artists may be despairing. But hunger artists also are very stubborn. If this is your affliction, where you may be stubbornly holding on to your lack of appetite, wearing it like a badge of honor, I would ask you to ceremonially drop the stubbornness, even though what you may then encounter is the pain you have been studiously trying to avoid. If you can't quite drop the stubbornness all at once, then at least engage with this little exercise.

Read through the following list of "Ten Tips" and see if you can stay open to the idea that unless you can find your appetite for creating, you won't create. There is nothing for you to "do" with any of the following tips. I am hoping that together they amount to a kind of tipping point, when, all of a sudden and maybe for the first time, you begin to understand the connection between the various synonyms I'm using and the odd challenge you are facing.

1. **Get obsessed.** The word *obsession* got co-opted by the mental health world and was turned into a negative by definition. When you define obsessions as "intrusive, unwanted thoughts," then naturally all obsessions are negative. But not every repetitive thought is unwanted or intrusive. Some are exactly the thoughts we want. One way to fall back in love with your work is to allow yourself to obsess about it, to bite into it, to think about it, to pay attention to it.

2. **Become a little more impetuous.** You may be living your life in as careful, controlled, and contained a way as you can so that you make sure you take care of all your responsibilities

and get every item checked off your perpetual to-do list. That way of living can be entirely appropriate, but it pretty much bars the door on impetuosity. Try being more impetuous both with your art and your art career. Impetuously get up from whatever you are doing and go write. Impetuously drop a gallery owner in London an e-mail that introduces you to them. Impetuously write a song "out of the blue." In the family of words that include *love, passion,* and *appetite, impetuous* is an important one.

3.  **Want appetites.** We rein in our appetites for all sorts of reasons: so that we don't gain too much weight, so that we don't have affairs and betray our mate, so that we don't drive too fast and get too many speeding tickets. Rather than reining in all of your appetites, just rein in those that produce negative consequences. Let yourself be really appetitive when it comes to your creating and your art. In those areas, let yourself feel hungry!

4.  **Be ambitious.** Sometimes we sell ourselves on the idea that it is unseemly to have ambitions and that ambitiousness is a manifestation of

narcissism or pride. It is nothing of the kind. To have ambitions is to want things, to have desires, to have passions. It is perfectly proper to have desires and passions and want things like best sellers or gallery shows or articles written about you or anything of that sort. Try to free yourself from the idea that there is something wrong with being ambitious, as those ambitions are  manifestations of desire—and desire is a good thing!

5.  **Feel devoted to your work.** The late Luciano Pavarotti has a quote that I like and that I often repeat: "People say that I'm disciplined, but it's not discipline. It's devotion. And there's a big difference." There is. We are in a completely different relationship to our art when we feel devoted to it as opposed to when we feel it is something that we "should" be doing. If you have never felt devoted to anything, you may want to try to locate that feeling in your being and start to treat your art as an object of devotion.

6.  **Opt for intensity and even exhaustion**. One of the ways that we honor our pledge to make personal meaning is to do the work required of

us, even if that effort exhausts us. If it exhausts us, then we rest. But we do not let the fear of exhaustion prevent us from making our meaning. You might start painting at sunrise and go until midnight, getting tired, confused, anxious, frayed, sad, and whatever else befalls you as you struggle to create. When, after many hours of doing battle, you can't muster another thought or another brushstroke, you may want to scream, cry, or feed the cat, but do not even think about throwing in the towel. Try to live that intensely. Exhaust yourself in the service of your work and then reward yourself, at the very least with the compliment "I worked hard, I didn't fall apart, and I'm proud of my efforts."

7. **Understand the power of our cultural and societal injunctions against passion.** Those injunctions can easily stop you from expressing the passion you feel. We are a very buttoned-down, nonexpressive, don't-let-your-emotions-show kind of culture, and everyone is infected by that cultural trance. It can feel very hard to go against the grain and

act passionately in the service of your own ideas and projects. If you know that you are somehow inhibited by cultural messages and the demand not to look conspicuous, try to think through what you can do to shed that cultural straitjacket.

8. **Remember that passion isn't unseemly.** We have to get it out of our head that there is something wrong or unseemly about being passionate, being obsessed, or being in love with our work. If we are holding a mental injunction against passion or an internal lack of permission to be passionate, that will severely restrict our ability to create.

9. **Remember that passion isn't a given.** You have to bring the passion, the appetite, the desire. It won't just appear by virtue of your showing up at the canvas or the computer screen. You need to bring enthusiasm and passion with you, which you do by actively falling back in love with your project, by investing meaning in your project, by thinking thoughts that serve you. Passion is not a given. You must bring it.

10. **Remember that passion and appetite aren't
    optional.** We have very little mental energy
    for something that bores us, for something
    that barely interests us, for something whose
    hardness outweighs its desirability. If we hold
    our work as difficult and think that what we
    need is a white-knuckled discipline to get to it,
    we won't get to it. If, instead, we hold our work
    as something we love and something to which
    we are devoted, we will get to it. The addition of
    love will make all the difference in the world.

## Holiday Cards and Refrigerator Magnets

No client is more frustrating to work with than the one
with no appetite. They are often the most pleasant and
agreeable—and the most stubborn. They are regularly
adamant in announcing that, yes, something is wrong, but,
no, nothing is really wrong. And, yes, they might certainly
do this or that, but, no, unfortunately there are reasons
why they can't possibly do this or that. They give with
one hand and take back with the other, always mildly, as
if they hadn't a care in the world—or as if nothing really
mattered.

I was speaking with a new client, Jill, via Skype. In her introduction, she explained that a long time ago she'd gotten a BFA and an MFA in painting, but then children arrived and she'd never really pursued her art. What she wanted was to be "a little creative every day," which she thought might mean doing crafts projects with the children in connection with the holiday season. This was a red flag, as it was hard to see why crafting with her kids required the help of a creativity coach. But I supposed that there was more going on here than met the eye.

After the usual pleasantries, we began.

"So you'd like to do craft projects with your kids?"

"That might be nice," she said, without the least trace of energy or enthusiasm.

"Help me here. You have a BFA and an MFA. But you don't want to paint?"

"Oh, I wouldn't mind painting. But the kids are so young."

"I'm not quite following," I said. "That they are so young is a problem because . . . ?"

"Well, I'd have to set up a dedicated studio for the painting and they'd want to get in there."

"You could rent studio space away from the house, yes?"

"Oh, I don't have time for that." She smiled pleasantly. "Plus, the children are so young."

We continued on, chatting about the crafts projects she had in mind. Contemplating creating holiday cards and refrigerator magnets did not seem to be stirring her blood much. I wondered out loud if there was anything that might be interesting her *more*. I poked about for a bit but was met with stubborn, albeit pleasant, resistance.

"So there's nothing you'd really like to do?"

"Oh no. I'd really like to make those holiday cards. And those magnets."

"And tell me again what's preventing you from doing that?"

"Nothing, really."

"So," I continued, "this week you'll make holiday cards and refrigerator magnets with the kids?"

"No. I don't have what I need. And I doubt that I can get to a craft store this week."

"So . . . what will you do this week?"

"I could straighten out the craft room."

"So . . . that's what you'll do?"

She shook her head. "Probably not this week. There are so many things in there waiting to be used for the holiday season, I wouldn't know where to put them."

"I don't think I quite understand. You do have the supplies in there, waiting to be used?"

"Oh, I have lots of things in there! All sorts of things. Just not the right things."

A coach can't just come out and say, "You have no interest in making those cards or those magnets, do you?" Although speaking that bluntly might prove productive, it's nevertheless too critical and too insulting an approach, certainly in a first session. If we'd had a relationship built over time, I might have said that—with a smile in my voice, of course. But as it was, I had to bite my tongue and find a place to continue.

"Is there a small thing in the service of your creative life that you could do this week?" I wondered.

"I could look at the work of artists I like. I'd enjoy that."

"Do you have an artist in mind?"

"No. I don't think I've looked at my art books in fifteen years. They're all in the garage in boxes."

"But you could search your memory and remember an artist you like? And then look him or her up on the Internet or in a good library?"

"I could do that."

"Is that something you'd like to do this week?"

"I could do that."

We continued, arriving nowhere in particular. We could not have left matters in a less promising state. Jill, however, announced that she was very happy with the session and that it had helped her a lot. I wondered if I had. I wondered if I would get an e-mail from Jill, saying something to the effect of "I don't think that this is exactly the right time for me to be engaged in coaching." Two days later, a very different sort of e-mail came in. Jill reported that she had started the week with very low expectations, but that when she started looking at artists she loved, she found herself falling back in love with art. "I'm hungry again!" she reported. "Famished, really!"

If, being honest with yourself, you conclude that you do not have any real appetite for the creative work you claim you want to pursue, then you must either discern why you are not hungry, as painful as that excavating may be, or else demand of yourself that you engage in your creative work even though you aren't hungry for it, as heavy lifting as that may be. Do not be stubborn and smile a rueful smile and do nothing. Do not be a hunger artist instead of a working artist.

By tackling this matter head-on, you may discover that you're actually very close—*thisclose*—to making meaning again. I've seen that happen time and again. "Meaning," being a certain sort of psychological experience, is an infinitely renewable resource. Announce, "I am really, really hungry!" and partake of the feast that is waiting for you.

# Chapter 4

## RESTORING LOST MEANING

Artists are able to create and perform because they find those pursuits meaningful. What happens when the meaning leaks out of those pursuits and a meaning crisis ensues? This happens so often that it must be counted as one of an artist's most important challenges. When meaning goes missing and when what you are attempting to do no longer feels significant or important, how likely is it that you'll be able to unleash your creative potential?

Let's take a good, close look at meaning. Something is meaningful because we experience it as such. It is not meaningful "in its own right"; it is only meaningful *to me*. For one person, parenting is about as meaningful an experience as any can be. For another, parenting means nothing—they have no feeling for it, nothing about it stirs them, nothing about it connects to how they want to live life. Same with writing a novel or composing a symphony. To one person, writing a novel is a wonderfully meaningful activity. To another, it isn't at all. Meaning is a subjective psychological experience; it is not something "out there." It is something that you and I experience in our own ways.

Because meaning is a psychological experience, it is never a settled matter. It comes and goes, as moods come and go. Good mood, bad mood, up mood, down mood. Life can feel meaningful for a moment and then it can turn meaningless. Life can feel meaningful for a month, as you work with enthusiasm and excitement on new paintings and anticipate the gallery show you're about to have; then it can turn bleak, desperate, and meaningless when the show runs its course and not a single painting sells.

Life felt full to the brim with meaning as you painted. Then it felt emptied of meaning, progressively drained of it, as another day of your show passed without a sale. Meaning coming and going in this way happens because it is a thing of the mind, and the mind can change in an instant. One moment you love what painting can do. The next moment you find it absurd to care so much about pigments on canvas. One moment you love what a novel can do. The next moment you berate yourself for fiddling with words while the world burns. Meaning fills you up because of an aroma;

meaning flees because of a smell. You must understand this and get ready for it.

We are built to deal reasonably well with this taxing phenomenon. First, we can understand it rather than misunderstand it. Then we can opt for a single go-to answer: to live our life purposes. That is the complete answer to the tragic problem of meaning coming and going. We can assert the following first principle: "I'm not going to worry that much about meaning. I'm only going to live my life purposes. And if I do, meaning may well return, just as the sun is likely to come up tomorrow."

Know your life purposes. Live them. If meaning attaches, wonderful. If not, live your life purposes anyway. And if you suddenly doubt your life purposes? Then you have precipitated a meaning crisis. If you suddenly doubt that it is important to write your novel, then you will have killed off meaning in that domain. You will have sent it packing. You will have announced to yourself, "Well, I can continue scribbling but, of course, that's absurd and ridiculous now that I've peeked behind the curtain and seen that novel-writing means nothing to me." Your doubt will have opened the door to a loss of meaning.

Can you keep scribbling? Maybe. Maybe by dint of will or out of guilt or because you're under contract, you may be able to continue writing your novel. But will the experience feel meaningful? Not a chance. No way, since you yourself sent meaning packing. Should we say that the meaning was lost? Or should we say instead that meaning was banished? Something happened inside your mind. You made a new calculation and a new decision that novel-writing was no longer worth the candle, and you summarily lost a life purpose and meaning.

The short answer? Reinstate writing as a life purpose or choose to live another life purpose that is equal in weight and importance to the one you dismissed. Reinvigorate a former life purpose, live your other life purposes, or both! The solution to the problem of lost meaning is not to go on a hunt to find it. The solution is to live your life purposes and to presume, with fingers crossed, that meaning will return of its own accord. Presume that when meaning vanishes, it will return, if you have decided what your life purposes are and live them on a daily basis.

Will this simple recipe for the return of meaning— live your life purposes—work if your challenges are of the following sort? Maybe you don't really have any life purposes; maybe nothing has ever managed to rise to that high-bar place. Maybe you've received a blow that feels like a death knell to meaning: the death of a loved one, a tyrant taking over your nation, your personal failure for the hundredth time as you again abandon your creative work. Maybe nothing has ever felt particularly meaningful, and its coming and going isn't the issue. It's that meaning hasn't once visited you. Can "live your life purposes" stand as the go-to answer when you don't have any life purposes or you don't even know what meaning looks like or smells like? Yes, it is the go-to answer, made all the more difficult by the fact that you are trying to bring into existence something—a felt sense of purpose—that may never have arisen in you.

If you're smart, sensitive, and creative, you'll want to unleash all that potential. But the modern world is designed to restrict your options and straitjacket your efforts. There is no contemporary category of "general thinker" that matches the ancient job title of "natural philosopher," where one could do science, philosophy, art, and anything else that caught one's fancy. Nowadays you must do something much smaller than that.

The challenges that smart, sensitive, creative people face when it comes to finding meaningful employment—surviving dull, routine work; avoiding a lifetime in a claustrophobic corner of a given profession; choosing between work that pays and work that interests them; and generally adapting their smarts to the contours of society's configurations—are never-ending. No wonder that meaning routinely vanishes! You may prove to be one of the lucky ones, make an excellent match, and never feel straitjacketed in these ways. But as likely as not, you will find yourself among the majority of smart people who perennially find that the world is designed to restrict their thinking and restrain their talents.

Meaning is a deep, inexhaustible wellspring and an infinitely renewable resource. Today, it may not seem meaningful to sit by the pond and feed the ducks, as you have too much you want to do. However, sixty years from now— or tomorrow, for that matter—you may decide that sitting by the pond for an hour or two is abundantly meaningful. At nine in the morning, the meaning that springs to your mind might be to fight an injustice; at ten, to send your daughter at college a sweet note; at eleven, to work on the song you're writing; at noon, to stretch and write for another hour; at one, to pass on "the whole meaning business" and pay bills; and at two, to resume fighting that injustice. There is always more meaning available.

To think of meaning as something to find—something like a lost wallet or a lost ring—is to picture meaning as a very paltry thing indeed. Bob, a coaching client, explained to me, "I know nothing about ultimate reality, and I'm certain that no one else does either. But I recognize that some things feel meaningful to me and even consistently meaningful. If this is true, that is the same thing as saying that meaning is available to me. It may not be available to me at all times, in all moods, or in all weather, but I embrace the idea that meaning is a renewable human resource. More than that, I can take charge of it bubbling up. This may sound strange in words, but I know what I mean. I know how to accomplish this feat of restoring the meaning flow in my life."

Marcia, another client, explained to me: "As I began to really see that meaning is a wellspring, I felt more connected, hopeful, and empowered. I felt a sense of connecting not only to a particular meaning-making choice, but to a deeper awareness of the limitlessness of possible meanings and choices. I found myself at times visualizing journeying into a wellspring deep in the earth, traveling through time, traveling and shape-shifting into the awareness and viewpoints of other people, of animals, of trees, of energies that had taken a drink from the wellspring. These were like little creation stories. As soon as I internally agreed that meaning was a wellspring, it not only shifted my understanding of meaning-making but brought on a lightness as well."

Susan, a third client, put it this way: "Conceptualizing meaning as always available changed my relationship to meaning. Like Old Faithful, the famous Yellowstone geyser, I began arriving at my desk with a bubbling up of energy. I experienced a building sense of creativity during the days when, because of my other responsibilities, I couldn't get to my writing. Then, on the days when I could, I found myself able to stay put for much longer periods of time. The image of an inexhaustible wellspring helped me maintain meaning on the days when I couldn't get to the computer and it helped me make meaning on the days when I could. It seemed to work on many levels, to deepen my connection to my creative work, to banish existential depression, and to help me do the ordinary everyday things more lightly and effortlessly."

Deal with the poignant reality that meaning is bound to vanish by conceptualizing it as a renewable resource while living your life purposes. Here are nine tips in this regard:

1. **You decide to matter.** The universe is not built to care about you. You must care about you. You must announce that you are opting to matter. You must announce that you are making the startling eye-opening decision to take responsibility for your thoughts and your actions and for living your life instrumentally.

2. **You accept that you must make meaning.**
   You finally let go of the demoralizing wish
   that meaning rain down on you from a golden
   universal shower. Instead, you accept that the
   only meaning that exists is the meaning you
   make by virtue of living your life purposes.
   You announce once and for all that you
   are the final arbiter of meaning.

3. **You identify your life purposes.** If you are
   going to actively make meaning in accord-
   ance with your life purposes, you had better
   know what your life purposes are, articulate
   them, keep them up-to-date (because life
   purposes shift and change), and live them.

4. **You articulate a life-purpose statement.**
   You list your life purposes, rank order your life
   purposes, and then hold a single phrase with a
   clear understanding of how you intend to live
   your life and represent yourself in the universe.
   My life-purpose statement is "Do the next right
   thing." What's yours?

5. **You hold the intention to fulfill your life
   purposes.** You need to keep your meaning-
   making efforts firmly in mind. You must be

able to remember your life purposes even when you are tired, bothered, distracted, upset, and otherwise not in your best frame of self. When life resumes its habitual busyness, you must firmly hold your intentions and manifest them.

6. **You passionately act to fulfill your life purposes.** Every day you live one or more of your life purposes. Maybe eight hours of the day are robbed by activities that do not align with them and that you must attend to for all the usual reasons. But a few hours remain, and you must use them for your life purposes.

7. **You navigate the world and the facts of existence.** The world is not built to accommodate you. Your favorite bakery may close or war may break out. From the smallest to the largest, the facts of existence are exactly what they are. They include pleasure and pain, loyalty and betrayal, life and death. All of this you must navigate, right up until the final moment.

8. **You create yourself in your own best image.** You have indubitable strengths, and you also have ways that you sabotage yourself

and your efforts. If you engage in a lot of self-sabotage, you will never quite respect yourself. Do better than that by manifesting your strengths and by becoming the person you know you want to become. Be your best self.

9. **You live the life of a passionate meaning-maker.** You don't idly chat about meaning, brood about it, look for it, complain about it, buy a book about it, take a workshop on it. You live a life where, day in and day out, you make meaning. You wait on nothing. You live!

## Puppets, Headaches, and Life Purpose

Alena, a client of mine and a puppeteer and performance artist living across from the Prague castle park known as Vysehrad, had spent two decades upholding the Czech tradition of activist puppet theater.

She'd created touring companies; had performed in small theaters, in warehouses, and on street corners; and had even staged "puppet assaults" on business boardrooms and government offices. Now she was ready to throw in the towel. Her life had grown too hard, her income had grown too small, and her love of puppets had vanished.

I happened to be in Prague, leading a writing workshop and presenting on the subject of creativity and business at the American Chamber of Commerce. We made a date to meet at a beer garden in Vysehrad. There, she explained her situation.

"You've seen those remaining puppet shops scattered around Prague?" she began. "They mean nothing to me. Puppets for tourists! Movie stars. Pop singers. Dead princesses. Really? I need to get out of here!" She put her hand to her head.

"Headache?" I said.

"Terrible headaches. Migraines. This one isn't so bad. The doctors know nothing." She shook her head. "You and I have talked about my next steps. I know that I don't want to write a book about my experiences—no puppet memoir! That feels static and dead to me. I don't want to create pop-up performance pieces where I stand on Charles Bridge and do something 'in your face' and have tourists look at me like I'm ruining their day. I don't want to return to painting and turn out canvases that no one wants. Even if they wanted them, that feels dead and tired too. I need something different! But when I think of anything 'in the arts,' I feel tired, like none of that has any future."

We sat in the sun, nursing our beers.

"Is there a test to run to see if puppets are still important to you?" I wondered.

She thought about that. "Here are the tests that wouldn't work, that would prove nothing," she said after a while. "I could put on a show for my nieces, and they would love it, and we would all laugh, and I would enjoy that experience, but that wouldn't prove anything—only that puppets will be able to entertain children until the end of time." She shook her head. "I already know that. No, that 'test' would prove nothing—and would just make me sad."

She thought some more. "I could create a show and perform it in a club and have small audiences and limited success and that wouldn't prove anything one way or another, not even if the audiences were large and the show got attention."

"Not even then?"

"No. I know what that feels like, and it's not enough. Plus, it would lose me money. I can sometimes talk myself into believing that that is enough, but not this time. It's not enough."

I nodded.

"Let's say that I could manage to get interviewed on a big radio show," she continued, "and had an intelligent conversation with the host about the traditions, the magic, and the importance of puppeteering in Czech history. That would feel good. I would enjoy that. But it wouldn't amount to a test. I wouldn't learn anything from that, about whether or not I ought to continue, that I don't already know. That would amount to a nice one-off moment."

We sat in silence.

"The only 'test' that would reveal anything worth knowing," she said quietly, "would be to actually do the thing I believe can no longer be done and that I believe I no longer want to do, whatever that is, and see if doing it felt like it mattered. Which is kind of absurd—that the test is the act itself. I've already described the many, many reasons why I shouldn't do that. I can't afford it. It feels scary. It might be beyond my capabilities. I'm tired of doing such things alone. I'm three-quarters bored by the whole idea. And at the end of it, I will just be older. So when I say that the 'test' is to do it, what exactly am I saying? I don't know."

We continued and made progress. After about an hour, we had a tentative plan. Alena would create a "menu of meaning opportunities" that did not include any puppet-related or art-related activities, unless those activities arose powerfully and spontaneously as she was creating her list. Then we would meet again to see what wanted to appear on her list and what she learned. Because I was teaching the next day, we decided to meet late in the afternoon at a café near the Chamber of Commerce, directly across from the new Franz Kafka statue and around the corner from the Maisel synagogue.

Alena shook her head as she got seated. She didn't have a list with her.

"I've been fighting about moving into the current moment," she began. "The current moment is technology and the Internet, not small puppet stages in deserted parks. The puppets always had two meanings for me: as something genuinely magical and as a vehicle for activism. They no longer feel magical to me, and that's part of this long sadness I've been experiencing. But fighting for things does matter to me, even though I'm tired. So here's what I want to do, although I don't know what the following sentence means. I want to use the Internet for activist purposes, and I also want to make money at the same time because I'm tired of being so poor. That—to dignify a completely unformed idea—is my plan."

We grew silent. What did her "plan" really mean? I watched her rub her temples.

"Headache?" I said.

She nodded. "Bad."

I had several busy days ahead of me, and we made a date to meet on Sunday at a café in an out-of-the-way park. I got there early. When she arrived, Alena had with her a couple of friends, Ricky, a Brit, and Eugene, a Czech.

"We are a start-up!" Alena exclaimed. "Really, I just like saying that. I am 'starting up,' as in restarting my engine!"

"We aren't precisely sure what we're selling," Eugene said, "but we know that the puppets will do the selling! We'll have short videos of puppets pushing our ideas, and I guarantee that some of those puppet videos will go viral and drive people to our site. Some silly puppet thing called 'The Mysterious Ticking Noise' got 140,000,000 views! And Alena's puppets are wonderful. We are going to have billions of views!"

I smiled. "But you don't know what you're selling?"

"That's the easy part!" Eugene said. "It's all about magic and buzz and Alena's puppets!"

"I think my puppets have been ready for the twenty-first century for a long time," Alena said. "I just haven't been. I've been trapped in this time warp of my youth and of past centuries. But this feels exciting."

"And we will make money!" Eugene chimed in.

"Even though you don't know what you're selling?" I laughed.

"Alena's puppets can sell anything!" Eugene exclaimed.

I was watching Alena. She hadn't rubbed her temples once since she'd arrived.

"The headaches?" I asked.

"Completely gone!"

Two months later we did a Skype session.

"An organization in Berlin wants us to put on an Internet puppet campaign for their refugee relief efforts," Alena said. "They have the backing of the United Nations and private companies, and there's actual money. We're going to do it."

I had to ask. "And the headaches?"

"A thing of the past," she said. "And good riddance!"

Alena had gotten lucky. But in the realm of meaning, you can make your own luck. When the meaning drains out of what you are doing—when you can no longer get the psychological experience of meaning from your creative efforts—then your creative potential is bound to remain as potential only. To unleash it, you must actively work to restore meaning. The steps I described earlier in this chapter can aid you in that effort.

# Chapter 5

## RECOVERING FROM DASHED HOPES

The relationship between meaning and hope is a simple one. A setback that sends meaning packing will send hope packing as well. If your day job is draining the life out of you and you hate the fact that you have to put in forty hours a week at meaningless, menial work, how can that situation not make you feel hopeless? If your self-published mystery series, which it turns out is too light to sustain your own interest, has become more of a drudgery than a joy, that is bound to affect you, both on the level of meaning and hope.

Hope is no small commodity. In the absence of hope, you are left with despair. Therefore, if hope is absent or in short supply, restoring it is of pivotal importance. When the French novelist and existential writer Albert Camus painted a smile of victory on the face of his famous character Sisyphus, who had been condemned by the gods to roll stones up a mountain for all eternity but who nevertheless smiled at his predicament because he could still thumb his nose at his fate, Camus was not being true to life. In real life, human beings rarely smile when hope is stolen from them.

A loss of hope ruins our mental health. Existential thinkers have characteristically provided two answers to this dilemma: rebel by thumbing your nose at the facts of existence; and hope anyway, even though hope is absurd. These answers satisfy us in the corner of our being that appreciates irony and rebellion, but they hardly work as effective answers in the face of real, deep, abiding feelings of hopelessness.

If your mental health requires that you maintain hope and if you find yourself no longer believing that hope makes any sense, what can you do?

One small but nevertheless useful effort you can make is to create a hope chest that you keep in the room that is your mind. Either regularly or at the very least when you are feeling hopeless, visit your hope chest and ask the question "What in here can I hope for?" and cross your fingers that you will land on something that rekindles hope. You might discover that . . .

- You can hope for love.
- You can hope to love.

- You can hope for the small enjoyments that you have always enjoyed.
- You can hope to stand up for your principles and make a tiny difference in the world.
- You can hope to fight the enemies of reason.
- You can hope to wrestle something beautiful into existence.
- You can hope that your efforts will bring a few people small comfort or joy.

Ask yourself the question "Have I lost hope?" and honestly answer it. If you discover that you have indeed lost hope, go directly to the room that is your mind, create a hope chest, and fill it with as many talismans of hope as you can contrive. What will you include? Photographs? Quotations? Memories? Prophecies? Bark from a cherry tree? A miniature particle accelerator?

Make your talismans gigantic, tiny, ephemeral, solid, anything you need them to be. This is your hope chest to fill as you like and as you require. Spend time with these talismans. Losing hope regularly happens. If you've lost hope, you have the job of restoring it.

What will likely help the most is remembering to live your life purposes. There is no substitute for actively living your life purposes and no better way to restore hope. The first step in this restorative process is to identify what's important to you. What are your life purposes? Maybe among them are the desire to live ethically and authentically. Maybe you see activism, being of service, intimate relationships, manifesting your creative nature, having a career, your physical and emotional health, and healing from trauma as all important to you. These, then, are your life-purpose choices: your decisions about what matters to you. You get to decide. You are obliged to decide. Because until you decide you are, in effect, living without purpose.

Most people never consciously decide what's important to them. Indoctrinated in a way of thinking that makes the "purpose of life" seem extrinsic, as something out there, they aren't helped to understand that life-purpose choosing is an activity that they must engage in, a subjective reckoning about what's important and about how they intend to make themselves proud in life. When, finally, they understand that they must stand up and get behind their own choices, then each day has a chance to feel meaningful and each day comes with a ray of hope.

What if nothing feels particularly important? That is a horrible existential crisis, which many people are currently enduring. The main feeling that accompanies such a crisis is despair, and the main activity that accompanies such a crisis is going through the motions. Sad and bereft of hope, you do the next thing on your to-do list and the next thing after that, managing to get to the end of the day somehow. That is not the way you want to live. You must do the following two things:

1. **You must proclaim something as important.**
   This sounds like "I am picking my life purposes!" Whether or not your choices *feel* genuinely important, you must *proclaim* them as important. Yes, this is a kind of game. But it is a game on the side of life.

2. **Agree to play the game of life.** Decide to matter. Make your choices and then honor them by living them. Yes, you are clear-eyed enough to see through to the void and to the end of your time on earth. Yes, this enterprise of choosing and living your life purposes is rightly accompanied by some ironic laughter. All of that notwithstanding, this is the way to live: to announce your life-purpose choices and to live them.

Doing this will restore hope.

It is painfully easy for smart, sensitive, creative people to begin to doubt that they or any of their efforts really matter. Why spend so much time, sweat, energy, and blood crafting a poem? Why throw all of your intellectual eggs into the basket of string theory when string theory may prove a passing fancy? Why turn over your whole life to literary criticism when the books you are teaching bore you? Why provide another mental disorder diagnosis to another client when you've stopped believing in the logic or legitimacy of diagnosing? Why bother with any of this?

This common problem—a sense of lost purpose, the experience of encroaching meaninglessness, and a consequent loss of hope—is best counteracted in the following way. Remind yourself—or perhaps inform yourself for the first time—that you do not intend to make the mistake of believing that there is a single "meaning to life" or a single "purpose to life." Rather, go back to the idea that there are multiple life-purpose choices that you might make. Then announce that you are perfectly capable of doing a beautiful job of identifying a life-purpose choice to embrace when another life-purpose choice (for example, your current creative project) feels stale and empty.

If, today, writing poetry does not feel especially meaningful to you, decide to embrace your life-purpose choice of relationship and go to the zoo with your daughter; or embrace your life-purpose choice of service and volunteer your time; or embrace your life-purpose choice of activism and engage in smart work of a cause that matters to you. Quickly and clearly decide to embrace a life-purpose choice that feels alive and available. Then, tomorrow, you can see if returning to your poetry, your string theory, your literary criticism, or your clinical practice feels less dull and less beside the point. It may, indeed, because you've taken a vacation from it and spent time with a different meaningful pursuit.

To help remind yourself, try the following exercise:

1. **In your mind's eye, create a set of life-purpose china** that you store in the room which is your mind and which you use for existential snacking. Say that writing poetry has started to feel pointless. Go to the room that is your mind, move to the cupboard you have installed, and pull out your life-purpose china, the full set of them, the eight or ten or twelve life-purpose dinner plates that make up your complete service.

2. **Next, take a moment** (or however long you need) and think through what dozen motifs you want displayed on your dinner service. That is, see if you can create a menu of life-purpose choices. On that list might be important "doing" activities like creating, relating, serving, and truth-telling

and equally important "ways of being" states like calm, passionate, and authentic. Your choices might include "my health," "speaking up for children," "supporting my mate's career," or "moving evolutionary theory forward." Create your list or menu now.

3. **Lay out the plates**, each hand-painted with one of your life-purpose choices, and choose one for your upcoming snack. Maybe you'll choose your activism plate, your mystery-writing plate, your career plate, your friendship plate. Maybe you'll choose your "being calm" plate or your "being passionate" plate. Pick a plate, get out silverware, and prepare to snack.

4. **Mentally bring out your scones, butter, and jam.** Fix yourself a lovely snack on the life-purpose plate you've chosen. As you partake, daydream about how you intend to live that particular life purpose today. Will you take your daughter to the zoo? Ah, it's too chilly for that. Then might you take her on a visit to an art museum? That might be fun! You could teach her all about drawing outside

the lines and speaking in her own voice. That
would make for a lovely few hours. Do exactly
that and take her on that excellent field trip!

It is easy to forget the extent to which creating is not just
about making new or beautiful things, but also represents
one of your life-purpose choices. It's also easy to forget that
you have many other life-purpose choices available to you, in
addition to creating. Your set of life-purpose china, each plate
decorated with a different life-purpose choice, can provide
an important reminder on that score, aid you in maintaining
your existential good health, and help keep hope afloat.

Most artists experience fewer marketplace opportunities
than they want or need. As a result, they lose hope of ever
making it. They may go through the motions of selling,
sending out the occasional query to a literary agent, or
renting the occasional booth at a crafts fair, but such efforts
are accomplished half-heartedly, with zero enthusiasm, and
with little or no hope for a positive outcome.

Then, once in a blue moon, an excellent opportunity may come their way. And what if that rare and precious
opportunity nets little or nothing? That pain is truly tremendous. Having waited so long for something good to happen,
finally getting what looks like a breakthrough opportunity,
and having that too amount to nothing is too much to bear.

You finally manage to get your novel published, the editor loves it, there is all this buzz and fanfare, and the book sells poorly and vanishes almost instantly. You produce your own album and manage to get an interview on a nationally syndicated show, fully expecting that the interview is bound to generate sales and lead to something great. And nothing happens. The day after the interview is exactly the same as the day before. What a letdown!

How is an artist to deal with the reality that even marketed, promoted, and hyped events may produce meager results? How can you be resilient in the face of that? It is one thing to never succeed, but it is its own terrible, trying experience to *almost* succeed. Isn't that bound to kill off hope for all time?

## The Painter Who Fled to Provence

I'm reminded of a time in Paris. My wife and I are staying in the seventh arrondissement, about a block from the Boulevard Saint-Germain. My weeklong deep-writing workshop, held in the living room of the high-ceilinged apartment we are renting, has ended. I schedule a meeting with a client at the corner café. I am one of only three people—the painter, her Parisian gallery owner, and me—who know her secret: her recent solo show, attended by a thousand people including pop stars and tabloid celebrities, has sold nothing.

Anne has come in from Provence to meet with me. She has been hiding out there for months, licking her wounds, barely communicating with the world, and wondering if she can continue as an artist. The fact that she has previously sold paintings, that she has had successful shows, and that she has been something of a darling of the art world amounts to nothing. Not in the aftermath of what she has dubbed "that monumental disaster."

We meet over coffee. My goal is to help her change her perspective. Her career certainly took a hit. But for her to dwell on that "disaster" is a serious mistake and a recipe for despair. Focusing on that event is only one lens through which to look at her career. I quietly and carefully explain to her that she is fortunate to have had the successes she has had, that this one event may or may not signal anything or augur anything, and that her best path is to get on with her life and her art-making, the act of which, it turns out, has lost none of its luster for her.

I ask Anne to detach from the show results and invite a postmortem from the gallery owner. How brave that would be, to ask him why he thinks the show produced no sales! She isn't sure if she is equal to that, but I can tell she is thinking about it. Indeed, I can tell she is changing her mind even as we sit there, that she is getting over her wound and beginning to think about the future.

She lets slip that she is excited about new paintings she has in mind, paintings that she hasn't been able to begin, not while feeling demoralized. I can tell those paintings, rather than that "monumental disaster," are on her mind now. She is doing that thing which is the very best indicator that hope has returned. She is smiling. Nothing more clearly and poignantly signals the return of hope than a real smile.

"So will you be staying in Provence much longer?" I ask.

"I may be returning to Paris very soon," she says.

"To get back to work?"

"To get back to work."

"See if you can figure out what happened," I say.

"I don't want to know. But, of course, I also do."

"It may have been that the stars were misaligned," I offer. "Or who knows what."

"Or the paintings sucked."

"Or you are a misunderstood genius."

She laughs. "I'll vote for that one."

I get an e-mail from Anne a few days later. She has bravely met with the gallery owner and has had that painful conversation. It turns out that, in fact, Marcel has very little to offer by way of explanation. People "loved the paintings."

People were "wild for the paintings." Many expressed what Marcel feels was a completely genuine desire to make a purchase. Still, nothing sold. But, Anne explains with relief, Marcel is not down on her, has no intention of reducing her presence in his gallery, and has expressed his intention to redouble his efforts on behalf of her and her paintings.

Months later I hear from Anne that several paintings from the show have sold and that her new suite of paintings are progressing nicely. She is in excellent spirits. Well, almost. She still is facing all the challenges that creatives face regularly. But at least it appears that her "monumental disaster" has lost its sting and only occasionally comes back to haunt her.

No matter how real and profound the setback, an artist must do the work required to survive dashed hopes. To not do that work is to invite paralysis and collapse. There are first acts, second acts, and third acts. Artists may topple back down the mountain after a fleeting moment at the top, but they must dust themselves off at the foot of the mountain and announce, "I will still live with purpose."

I met Anne again a few years later. We both happened to find ourselves in Rome. I was leading another one of my deep-writing workshops and she was there for the opening of a show of her ceramic sculptures. She explained that her time in Provence had actually benefited her. While in the south of France, she had become acquainted for the first time with Picasso's ceramics. A seed had been planted. Alongside painting, she had begun to work in clay.

"I love it as much as painting," she said. "Which amazes me, because I always thought that painting was 'it.'"

"That's lovely, to have multiple loves." I laughed.

"Something about that Paris show allowed the ceramics a way in," she continued. "I had to reckon with the real possibility that my paintings might not be wanted, and so I must have said to myself that I had better create a backup plan if I wanted to continue as an artist. I didn't put two and two together until much later, but getting involved with ceramics was my backup plan."

Dashed hopes ruin lives. Anne was lucky. Although her hopes were briefly dashed, her prior successes, her resilience, her ongoing love of art-making, and my help allowed her to come back to hope again. You can go a long way toward making your own luck by deciding that you will not allow a setback to set you back too far. Yes, you may have to lick your wounds for a while, and, yes, you may lose your motivation to create. But if you keep reminding yourself that you intend to return and that it is your job to do so, you can come back—even to a place better than the one you found yourself in before.

# Chapter 6

## SUPPORTING RIGHT FEELING VIA RIGHT THINKING

For the sake of your creative life (and for the sake of your life in general), you likely want to feel a particular way: calm, say, or passionate, or cheerful. But do your thoughts support that intention?

There are two parts to the welcome outcome of calmness, passion, cheerfulness, or any other feeling that you may be desiring: the intention to nurture the feelings you want and the activity of thinking thoughts that support that intention. If you can make this a habit, holding that intention and thinking thoughts which support that intention, you will find yourself in a much better position to unleash your creative potential.

If you think thoughts like "I can't succeed," "I have no chance," "Who cares anyway?", "What's the point?", and similar thoughts, you prevent yourself from living your life purposes, creating among them, and you open yourself up to unwanted feelings like anxiety, boredom, and sadness. No skill is more important than learning to think thoughts that serve you.

This skill is two-pronged. First, when you think a thought that doesn't serve you, notice what you just said and instantly replace it with a thought that better serves you. For instance, you might suddenly think "I have no chance in life," which might be followed by a mood swing into despair or a behavior like pouring yourself a double Scotch or driving recklessly.

If you are practicing the skill of right thinking, the instant you hear yourself say "I have no chance in life," demand of yourself that you say "No, that thought doesn't serve me!" Then think a thought that better serves you. For instance, "I am adamant about succeeding" or "I absolutely do have a chance!" Notice that you are saying "That thought doesn't serve me," rather than "That thought isn't true." This is hugely important and prevents you from getting hijacked by true thoughts that, while true, don't serve you.

The second prong is to actively think thoughts that serve you on a regular basis, as part of your practice of right thinking. You might, for example, wake up each morning and say to yourself, "I am living my life purposes today."

Follow that thought with "I'm practicing calmness today" and "I'm loving my children today." In this way, by choosing the thoughts you intend to think and by then thinking them in a practiced way, you begin to extinguish ones that haven't been serving you and do yourself a world of good.

Sometimes the thoughts that aren't serving us are so muffled that we don't quite hear them, although we hear them just enough to upset ourselves. Or they pass by so quickly that we don't quite realize that we had a suspect thought, though now our mood has worsened or we suddenly feel unmotivated. Because both of these aspects of thinking regularly derail us—these whispered thoughts that we don't quite hear and these rapid thoughts that zip on by and leave a terrible residue—we have to learn to hear those muffled ones and register those quick ones. Only if we hear them and register them can we dispute them and replace them with thoughts that do serve us.

You can see that right thinking is real work. You need to be disputing thoughts that don't serve you the instant they bubble up. You need to be introducing thoughts that do serve you via the regular practice of right thinking. You need to be listening for those terrible almost-silent thoughts and noticing those painful fleeting ones. This is literally a full-time job, because you are always thinking thoughts and they need to be monitored. One stray thought can trigger a flood of emotions or a dark mood, which is why real vigilance is required.

Connected to this is the following idea: you want to think fewer "small" thoughts, the ones that needlessly grab neurons, that prevent you from thinking your "big" thoughts, and that, because you aren't managing to think your larger thoughts, ruin your mood.

You have to recognize the following: that minding a worry as if you are minding an infant, such that the worry is never far from your conscious awareness and that losing sight of it, even for an instant, causes you to scurry around the apartment searching for it, is not an innocent neurotic handicap but a complete self-theft program. It is the perfect way to steal billions of neurons from your meager many billions, leaving you that much duller and less imaginative. How clever is that?

A famous Zen parable, slightly mangled in the retelling, goes as follows: Master and disciple are out walking. They come to a deep, fast-rushing stream and encounter a damsel in distress who, perhaps because she prefers not to get her skirt wet, is stuck on this side of the stream. She asks the master to carry her across. Because of the ascetic tradition that they practice, the disciple presumes that the master will say no.

Lo and behold, the master agrees and carries her across. Master and disciple proceed on their merry way, the disciple brooding about (or envious of) the fact that his teacher got to touch a lady. Back at the monastery, the disciple confronts the master, exclaiming, "How could you do that? We are expressly forbidden from touching a woman!" The master smiles benignly (or else whacks him with a stick—I forget) and replies, "Are you thinking about that woman? I left her at the riverbank and, look, you are still carrying her around!"

The master got on with creating his next haiku. His student, by contrast, looks doomed—until he is enlightened or a little smarter—to turn over billions of his neurons to brooding about his master's conduct and parsing the distinction between an injunction against touching and the offer of a helping hand. Probably another few billion of his neurons will get devoted to fantasizing about that woman. The disciple is unable to empty his mind, a task that is the exact equivalent of freeing all those neurons and inviting them to return neurons to the fold.

A free neuron, unencumbered by the demand to do work—to connect with its buddies in the service of remembering how many spouses a certain celebrity has cycled through or to link in a sad daisy chain of remembrance about the time we didn't get that red bicycle—is an *available* neuron, quiet as a church mouse. Hence, the experience of profound silence that comes with "quiet mind." If you can get all or most of your neurons back, you will have acquired the silence and presence that attracts leaps of imagination.

Too many stolen neurons and you aren't actually present. Yes, you look like a writer, sitting there in front of your computer, chewing on your nail, and playing with a swell word whose lilt charms you. But it is only your body and a too-small percentage of your brain that you've brought to the task.

Your ability to create and to feel emotionally well are both contingent on your thinking thoughts that serve you and on your freeing neurons from unnecessary tasks. You say that you are intending to write, and certainly part of you means that. But a hundred million neurons are gripping the weather forecast. Another hundred million are holding your upset about running out of breakfast cereal. Another several hundred million are linked together to remind you that the first sentence you write today will prove that you are an idiot and an imposter. Most of the neurons you own are charged with a task or other, and the remaining few can't help but whimper, "You want *us* to dream up a great novel?"

There is a lot of delicate, delectable material up there in your head, neurons and synapses and neural transmitters and all sorts of fancy machinery that the universe has gone to a lot of trouble to create so that *you* could create. Don't waste it by turning neurons over to tasks that are the equivalent of getting your socks matched. Every freed neuron is a tiny fraction of a great idea, and only you are its liberator.

Let's segue now to the matter of your emotions. You get angry. You get envious. You get sad. You are not a stone. Nor do you want to be. You have no intention of not feeling. You have no intention of taming your emotions so well that you end up domesticated and limp. You want your full measure of emotion because it is the lifeblood of art. Emotion is the surest sign that you are alive, the deepest motivator, and the edge that causes your knife to cut. Of course, you intend to live with emotions. But that doesn't mean you must live as a slave to them.

Say that you hear about a writer getting a big advance. Do you want to feel bad for a week or do you want to let that pain go? Say that an editor criticizes your short story. Do you want to writhe in agony or dismiss her criticism with a laugh? Say that you've had nothing published for two years. Do you want to sink into despair or demand of yourself continued optimism? In each case, you should want the latter from yourself. There is no good point in allowing your feelings to rule you as if you were a rag doll puppet.

If you think that is too tall an order, think again. Remember the time you decided you didn't want to feel a certain way any longer and felt better instantly? I'm certain you've had that experience. Now, from today on, you will endeavor to replicate that experience: you will let go of unwanted feelings as quickly as possible, sooner rather than later.

All the emotions that sometimes get you down—the pain, discouragement, bitterness, self-disgust, rage, sorrow, emptiness, hollowness, envy, fear—may well rear up automatically and reflexively in response to a stimulus. But in the next split second, the emotion having arrived, you get to decide whether you will embrace it and invite it to stay or whether you will meet it with mindful resolve and show it the door.

Think thoughts that serve you, free neurons from their grip, and let go of unwanted emotions. That's your job. If you know it will rile you to reread that curt e-mail from a literary agent, delete it. What are you saving it for? To upset yourself? For the day when exactly the right retort will come to your mind and you can get even? Delete it. Let it go. That is the self-beneficial thing to do. That is the mindful thing to do. Do not save bile as if it were fuel for the winter.

If you embrace your bilious emotions, cherish them, take pride in them, and keep them warm, chances are you'll find yourself making one mess after another. There is always a cost to raging, to tempests, and to black moods. Words like *sanguine* and *phlegmatic* are not the most exciting words in the dictionary, but they are nevertheless golden. Become someone who is able to mind one's emotions: that is an integral part of the program to unleash your creative potential and live well.

Sometimes you may want to hold firmly on to your rage. Sometimes you may want to sink into a well-earned funk. Sometimes you may want to feel exquisitely fearful and shiver for your life. There are moments when even our darkest emotions have a place, and there are good reasons for feeling bad on occasion. But it is not a healthy way of life. Limit your darker emotions as you limit your intake of chocolate: just like a little sweet goes a long way, so does a little sour.

People engaged in right thinking and right feeling don't strive to avoid feeling and don't hope against hope that unwanted feelings will stop arising altogether. Rather, they monitor their emotions and master them by embracing the ones they want and discarding the ones they don't. This isn't an easy practice, but it is an invaluable one. So try the following. The next time you get angry this week, decide not to be angry. The next time you get morose this week, decide not to be morose. The next time you get envious this week, decide not to be envious. The next time you experience any emotion this week, embrace it or discard it. It's your choice.

I ask the creativity coaches I train to try out the preceding exercise. Here's Elizabeth's response:

"This week was a very stressful week, full of many adrenaline-rushed moments. My five-year-old finished pre-school three weeks ago, and my eight-year-old finished two weeks ago. I have been on a new routine and schedule getting the kids to camp and classes while teaching every day, and we were scheduled to leave to visit family on Friday.

"I needed to remain extremely organized to make sure that everything got completed on time. I had to tackle a new task every day: the laundry, cleaning out the refrigerator, cleaning out the fish tank, house cleaning, and packing up everyone's clothes and items for the trip. I also needed to deliver the final to my college students on Thursday, grade all thirty-one essays (four pages each), and submit my final grades before leaving. And because the universe has an amazingly funny sense of humor, I was scheduled for jury duty Tuesday, which I didn't immediately get out of and had to continue calling in on standby all day.

"Needless to say, it was an extremely stressful few days leading up to the day we were leaving. Late Thursday night, I talked with my husband about our luggage and went to bed, having completed everything. But on Friday morning, my husband interrupted my workout to ask about something we had decided on a few hours earlier the night prior. He was presenting at a conference and was very stressed and seemed to be picking a fight. As he was venting, **somehow I remained calm.**

"I managed to stay on top of everything, and I arrived early to pick up my kids from their morning camp class. I had a lovely amount of time before I needed to pick them up, so I decided I was going to meditate in the car. But something told me to check my e-mail first. I found out our flight was two hours delayed. I had hoped to arrive on time because I had planned to see my best friend from high school, whom I hadn't seen in twenty years. Our flight being delayed meant I wouldn't be able to see her. Though I was extremely disappointed, **somehow I remained calm.**

"I had planned on having lunch with my mom when we arrived, but changed course to have lunch at home before we left for the airport. We were finally on our way, getting excited, when I again checked my e-mail, only to find out that our flight was canceled. Upset, I called my husband. He called the credit card company and learned that our travel insurance only covered delayed flights and not canceled ones. As I made my way to the charter airport, I was very upset—or, rather, thought that I was very upset—and told the kids that I was really upset and that they needed to be patient with me. I did lots of deep breathing in the car, and I discovered that I wasn't, in fact, really upset. **Somehow I remained calm.**

"The ladies at the ticketing counter helped us get on a new flight at the closest major airport, took care of our transportation there, and helped pack up the car. As we were leaving, the woman thanked me. She said I was so patient and understanding, whereas everyone else had been screaming at them all afternoon, saying that they had intentionally ruined their lives. She even commented on how well-behaved my children were. We ended up arriving to my hometown, with my mom greeting us nine hours after we initially were supposed to arrive. The thing is, I didn't think about this assignment: **'The next time you get angry this week, decide not to be angry.'** I didn't think about it until tonight, when I remembered that I needed to submit my response. But, somehow, I think I did remember.

"I had read the lesson on Monday, and maybe it did sink in. I laughed when I saw my mom waiting for us, and she wondered why I had a smile on my face after that ordeal. I told her all about the woman thanking me for remaining calm, and my mom laughed and responded, 'You?' She was as shocked as I was. I am not normally the calm person, not in any situation. I am like Ferdinand the bull. I want to be left alone to smell the flowers, but when you sting me, I uncontrollably get out of control. I would love to be the person who thinks before she speaks, but I have never been that person. But perhaps after this week's lesson, I can say that I have never been that person until now."

Elizabeth's report may not sound like it has anything at all to do with unlocking creative potential. But it does. If you think thoughts that serve you, free neurons from their grip, release them from both unnecessary thoughts and unwanted feelings, and hold the intention to shed yourself of unwanted emotions sooner rather than later, you are positioning yourself to make use of your creative nature. Plus, you will be living a healthier, all-around more satisfying life.

By thinking thoughts that serve you, you support your intention of cultivating the emotions you want. This two-way relationship between thinking and feeling, where right thoughts support right emotions and right emotions support right thoughts, is a key to achieving your creative goals. Like any healthy, well-functioning relationship, an excellent relationship between thinking and feeling requires hard work and serious attention. But if you manage to achieve it, it will absolutely pay dividends!

# Chapter 7

## CREATING AND RELATING

When it comes to dealing with the issues we've looked at so far—embracing the realities of process, restoring lost meaning, and recovering from dashed hopes—and when it comes to dealing with the issues we'll examine further along, the quality of your intimate relationships matters. That may not seem relevant at first glance, but let's look at the matter more closely.

You can certainly unleash your creative potential while avoiding intimate relationships. Countless creatives have done that. But living without the warmth and support of intimacy typically produces coldness and sadness. Yes, creatives need their solitude and their creative space and often prefer their own company. But human beings also yearn for and crave intimacy. If you would like to unleash your creative potential *and* enjoy life, then you might want to make intimate relating a priority. In my thirty years of working with creatives, I've found that clients benefit greatly from the warmth and support of a successful intimate relationship.

That isn't to say that intimate relating is easy or doesn't come with profound challenges. Creatives have all the relationship issues that confront other human beings—and special ones as well. What do these special challenges sound like in the real lives of creatives? Here are two characteristic complaints:

John, a sculptor, lamented, "Being married to an art director is tough. My wife is very outspoken and sometimes hurts my feelings with her comments or criticisms, thereby dulling my creative spirit. How do I get her to stop telling me what's wrong with my artwork and to start creating her own artworks once again? She is a very good artist in her own right, but she seems to need to control my creative efforts. I wonder if this need to control and criticize flows from her high-pressure career in the advertising industry?"

Marjorie, a mystery writer, explained, "I was engaged to a nice man once, but I couldn't go through with it. Why? He was unable or unwilling to give me any time alone to read, write, or engage in other artistic pursuits. I knew marriage wouldn't help matters. The man I marry doesn't have to be an artist, but he must appreciate my bohemian side enough to leave me alone for a set amount of time to do what I need to do. I will be glad to make it up to him afterward!"

For artists, many special factors enter the equation and make their relationship options more complicated. Like anyone, they would love their mate to be a friend, lover, partner, sympathetic ear, intimate, and soul mate. But they also have other special requirements. They need their mate to provide them with real freedom, the freedom to hold their own ideas, make artistic and human mistakes and messes, spend vast quantities of time in solitude, and, in a sense that inevitably stretches the fabric of relationship, live a fully independent life.

They also need their mate to appreciate their life project as an artist, that their commitment to the creative life is not "one of the things they do" but an imperative as real as breathing. Likewise, they need their mate to put up with their inevitably rich and roiling inner life, an inner life that manifests itself as dreams, nightmares, a sudden need for Paris, and a sudden desire to throw over painting for sculpture. To be sure, they may settle for a mate who does not meet these criteria, but if they do, they will experience the relationship as a settling.

They are also likely to have special survival needs because of the way our culture is constituted. If they could paint and pay their bills, they would not need a mate with a salary. Because so few artists in any of the disciplines can earn anything like a middle-class income, because typically there are only the extremes of poverty and celebrity, they are likely to be poor and to make certain mental calculations about how they might survive. One path, not always held consciously but nevertheless held, is to look for someone who, rather than choosing to manifest their creative potential, has gone into accounting.

Artists know that they are not entering a relationship of this sort with clean hands. By the same token, they may truly believe that there are enough good reasons in play to counterbalance their calculated decision. The person in question may be sweet, decent, charmed by the artist's life, happy to provide, and genuinely encouraging. Still, an artist's choice to opt for this kind of security is likely to come back to haunt them.

Conversely artists may say to themselves, "I will not choose a boring mate just because I could then get to paint," and may therefore choose their mate based on sympathetic resonances, which will likely be found in the being and body of a similarly impoverished artist. Then the endless dramas and negotiations can't help but begin: who will work the day job, who has the better prospects and is more entitled to a full shot at an art career, who will sacrifice for the other, and who will bite the bullet and go into the world when times are hard (which will be too often or even all the time).

The upshot is that many artists find themselves spending long periods of time alone, as their needs and requirements are not easily met by the people they encounter; in distant relationships, whose distance is a function of the basic incompatibility of the partners; in dramatic relationships, where each partner feels unjustly treated and makes that dissatisfaction known; in brief relationships, as their needs for intimacy collide with the fact that insufficient reasons exist for remaining with this or that partner; or in despairing relationships, where both partners feel emotionally and existentially under the weather.

Artists struggle as they try to balance their desire for relationship with the many real and perceived drawbacks of relationship. Some come to feel that they do best with a partner whom they see relatively rarely—and then wonder if that is really a completely satisfactory solution.

Coco, a performance artist, explained:

"An artist's desire to keep things interesting, alive, spontaneous, independent, and free: that's me. Those are exactly the reasons why I shy away from longer-term relationships or the idea of marriage. I'm not sure I'm capable of compromising any of those things, no matter how much I love the other person. I'm afraid of commitment because I know myself, and I know that I have a powerful need for change.

"Luckily my current partner, who is living halfway across the globe, feels exactly the same way. He is an artist who very much needs and loves his own space and independence. He, too, wants to know who he is and what his life would be like without the influence of a full-time partner. We love being together when we're together, and I feel lucky to have someone who is so like me and who understands my needs.

"I've noticed, though, that we never seem to be creative at the same time. He seems to be less inspired to do his work when he is with me. I feel like he is losing out on more when he is with me, no matter how much I encourage and support him. I do wish that our situation could be different and that we could be creative together. I would love one day to feel more like part of a team rather than on my own with a boyfriend who most of the time is thousands of miles away and who, when he's with me, is kind of itching to get away again."

The time to notice if a prospective partner is right for you is early on. Do they keep their word? Are they cavalierly cruel? Are they incapable of listening? Are they always rushing off and running around? Are their plans plausible or do they smack of wishful thinking? Do they do the simple things with grace and good cheer? Is everything a drama or an argument? Early on is the time to pay attention to such failings. If you notice them and do not heed them, well, you know the consequences of that.

One part of the relationship puzzle is choosing wisely. A mirror-image task is upgrading your own personality so that you are the sort of person you want to be and need to be, someone equal to the responsibilities of partnership. It is your duty to minimize your own unwanted qualities, whatever they are—your addictions, your unhealthy narcissism, your overly critical nature, your histrionics, your timidity, your lack of self-confidence, your arrogance, or whatever else it might be.

The necessity for a personality upgrade makes itself known in all the small and large bones of contention that partners encounter as they interact. These bones of contention are growth opportunities for you, if you take them as such. They allow you to begin to look in the mirror, take a fearless personal inventory, identify and then change those aspects of your personality that harm the relationship, and start the process of minimizing those qualities that you yourself decide ought to be changed.

Let's say that you agree you need a personality upgrade. How can you pull that off? It is exactly as simple and exactly as hard as admitting your drinking problem and entering recovery, seeing yourself in the mirror and beginning a diet and exercise program, listening to how you speak to yourself and beginning a regimen of more positive self-talk, or acknowledging that life makes you anxious and learning an anxiety management strategy or two that works for you. Upgrading is that simple and that hard. Countless books, workshops, and programs are available to you. The starting place is that magic sentence: "I need to work on this."

Let's say that both you and your partner want to work on upgrading yourselves. Excellent! Then you might try the following. Pick a quiet Sunday morning or another quiet time. Go your own separate ways: for instance one of you to a café and one of you to the library. There, have a written conversation with yourself and identify what you want to upgrade in your personality. Get the thing named clearly: "I want to begin to think thoughts that serve me";

"I want to increase my self-confidence"; "I want to reduce my arrogance and grandiosity." Then describe concretely what you intend to do over the coming two weeks to begin to accomplish your goal.

When you get home, have a celebration, celebrating your individual willingness to work on yourselves, but do not discuss your plans or intentions. Keep them private for now. Over the coming two weeks, do what you intended to do and arrange for a conversation at the end of that time when the two of you will visit and report. On, say, that Saturday night two weeks hence, explain what you have hoped to accomplish and report on what you, in fact, accomplished. If you got nothing done, ruefully admit that. Then announce your intentions for the next two-week period. Don't ask for suggestions or feedback, and don't offer suggestions or feedback. Just listen, nod, and smile. You are both working!

If, as a creative person, you would like to create a strong, long-lasting relationship with another human being, you almost certainly have areas of improvement, as, of course, does your partner. Make yourself proud by becoming the person you know you would like to be. If your partner doesn't also grow and change, that is on him or her. You have your own work to do, which will improve your relationship or make it easier for you to leave the relationship if your partner lags too far behind.

What, then, is required of two people, when one or both of them is creative, if they want a solid relationship? Here are sixteen keys:

1. **Be friendly.** Nothing is more crucial to the viability of an intimate relationship than the partners are friendly toward each other. Friendship, like love, requires its own sort of care and attention.

2. **Care for each other's solitude.** It must be more than all right for partners to spend significant amounts of time pursuing their own activities and communing with their inner life.

3. **Provide emotional security.** Each partner not only is aware of the other's feelings but takes them into account and actively works to help the partner feel good rather than bad.

4. **Meet meaning needs.** Partners understand that meaning comes and goes, that meaning crises will inevitably arise and require both partners' attention, and that identifying shared values and principles is a key to meaning maintenance.

5. **Maintain passion.** Partners will not let themselves become too busy, too tired, or too disinterested in love and intimacy.

6. **Gently demand discipline from oneself.** Each partner will strive to work in a productive, regular way, with few creative tantrums and excuses about not being inspired or in the mood.

7. **Gently exchange truths.** When there is something that must be said, it should be said carefully and compassionately, clearly and directly. A creative and his or her partner will want to speak honestly about the many large and small relationship matters that arise endlessly and that fester if not addressed.

8. **Accept difficulty.** While partners will naturally expect a lot from themselves and from each other, they also will recognize and accept that failures of nerve, black moods, and pratfalls do happen. Each partner will have a hard time of it some of the time.

9. **Minimize one's own unwanted qualities.** Each partner will bravely look in the mirror, take a fearless personal inventory, and identify

and then change those aspects of personality that harm the relationship.

10. **Support each other's career.** Each person in the partnership is likely to want and need a career in the arts and, hence, have career demands that need to be respected and negotiated.

11. **Manage one's own journey.** Each partner has the job of taking responsibility for his or her own life, for setting goals and planning, for making choices and taking action, and for proceeding as a responsible adult—of course, in consultation with one's partner.

12. **Bring one's artfulness to the partnership.** A creative person can bless their relationship by bringing the same qualities to it that they bring to their art, qualities as diverse as whimsy, imagination, resilience, and meticulousness.

13. **Maintain a present and future orientation.** Each partner lets go of past grievances, not to engage in wishful thinking or denial, but to deal with issues in their specific and current reality. And each partner likewise maintains hope for the future, both individually and for the couple.

**14. Treat each other fairly.** Fairness in everything —in the honoring of agreements, the equitable distribution of resources and opportunities, the respect shown in word and deed. Fairness is the glue that holds a healthy relationship together.

**15. Create at least occasional happiness.** Partners will actually ask questions of each other like "What would make us happy?" and "What would make you happy?" And when something would make them happy, they say so.

**16. Create a truly supportive relationship.** Even if two people find it easy to relate, even if both are "low maintenance," they will have to invest time and pay real attention to this thing they have created together, a real relationship.

The goal for artists and their partners is the creation by two ever-changing people of a bastion of safety and sanity in a dangerous world. It is the creation of a tight-knit unit, like a resistance cell in an occupied country, where each protects, supports, and respects the other. This fine relating eludes most artists and most human beings, but it remains the high ideal and the special prize worth pursuing.

# The Broken Window

When I first began working as a family therapist I decided to focus my practice on couples' work where one or both of the partners were creatives. In the San Francisco Bay Area, there was no shortage of such couples. When the couple was made up of a self-identified creative and a self-identified noncreative, typical complaints were that the creative, who rarely brought in any income, was a parasite; that the noncreative simply "didn't understand" the creative (and was also boring); that the noncreative was passive-aggressive, proclaiming support but acting anything but supportive.

In couples where both partners were self-identified creatives, typical dynamics included the following: a competitiveness that was muted on the surface but fierce underneath; anger and despair that leading creative lives produced; difficulties multiplied rather than reduced, by the fact that both partners were struggling to make it in their disciplines; envious feelings that made it hard to genuinely enjoy the other partner's successes.

The triggering crisis often was something relatively small. It might be that the supportive but actually passive-aggressive noncreative mate was supposed to pick up the partner at the airport but "got delayed" and kept them waiting for hours. It might be that one partner invited relatives to visit at the same time that the partner had an important art deadline looming. It might be that a partner was spending "too much money" on art supplies, studio space, or one's independent film. Issues of this sort would become the touchstone and lightning rod for the couple's electric antagonisms.

The following was a typical example. I was seeing a painter and a musician who were mad at each other because each felt that the other wasn't willing to take "just a little time off" to fix a broken window in their house. That was their current hot-button bone of contention: that the other was acting selfishly, cavalierly, and unfairly with regard to the "window thing." Where to start with this tangled issue? I began in a straightforward way: by looking at the exact nature of the window-fixing task.

I could tell that each of them was refusing to really add up how much time was involved in tackling this "little project," and so I had them lay out what was involved in fixing the window. It turned out that it was going to take one of them a dozen hours or more to get the job done. They had been denying this reality so as to be able to more easily charge the other with a relationship sin. We often "block" on tackling a project because we know that there are things that we have to learn, work that we have to do, and costs that we have to assume, and rather than admit and confess to all that, we refuse to honestly look at the task. My client couple was doing exactly that.

I forced John, the musician, and Stephanie, the painter, to sit still and add up the hours. Time spent traveling to and from the home supply store. Time spent learning how to replace a window, since neither one was very handy. Time spent returning to the home supply store because something got forgotten or something broke or something couldn't be fathomed. Time spent repainting the sash, if that was part of the project—and had they remembered to get touch-up paint? And did they know what color paint to order? And then cleaning up . . . They sat very quietly.

"Okay," I said, "do we agree that neither of you has been very real or fair about this?" They grudgingly agreed. "So let's try to get clarity around why you've been using this 'window thing' to level charges against each other. This bone of contention is a stand-in for the real problems in the relationship. What are they? Someone care to take a stab at that?"

John said nothing. After a bit Stephanie said, "We both feel behind the eight ball. Neither of us is doing as well as we would like, and we're using 'a lack of time' as the straw man. We both want more time in the day—which really means, we both want more good things to be happening in our careers."

This was the door opening. We could then begin to discuss what really mattered: that neither had the career that he or she wanted, and that, in order to have that career, both were going to need to improve their marketplace skills and increase their willingness to promote their wares. John was going to have to stop obsessing about whether one drummer or another drummer was best for the band and get on with the excruciating task of making money from his music. Stephanie was going to have to stop pestering herself about whether her current output amounted to two bodies of work or a single body of work and get on with the excruciating task of making money from her painting. Here was a clear place where they needed to upgrade their personality: they needed to become more willing and more capable salespeople.

"And what about the window?" I asked.

"The hell with the window!" John exclaimed.

"We'll reframe it as 'more fresh air!'" Stephanie laughed.

This was the happiest they'd been in a very long while. Then I asked the obvious question I'd held off asking all session.

"Why not hire a handyman to fix it?" I asked.

"Money," John said.

"Money," Stephanie said.

And so we had the next elephant in the room identified: how poor they were and how their lack of money ate away at their good spirits and kept them at each other's throats. This observation reinforced the theme that they were going to have to pay attention to their careers in new ways that would require their stretching far out of their current comfort zones.

It may seem at first glance that intimate relating hasn't much to do with unleashing one's creative potential. In one sense, it doesn't. A van Gogh can paint and a Beethoven can compose while shunning relationships. But van Gogh's suicide and Beethoven's despair remind us how cold life can feel without someone to talk with, make plans with, care about, hug, and love. And many creatives would not have been productive or able to unleash their creative potential without a supportive person in their lives. This may not be the easiest subject for you to think about, but I hope you can find the wherewithal to revisit that age-old question: "Might love help?"

# Chapter 8

## MANAGING THE DAILY GRIND

Free time is a true blessing for those in right relationship to their creative nature. It is much better to have the chance to write your novel than to have to drag yourself to a meaningless job five days a week—and then to spend the weekend recovering from a week's worth of nothingness while dealing with piled-up chores and errands. Not having to use all those hours at a daily grind is a blessing for those who are actually living their life purposes.

But even for someone with a burdensome day job or who is pressed by other daily responsibilities, like raising children or minding an aging parent, a lack of time is never the complete issue. One of the ways that blocked creatives and would-be creatives avoid doing their work is to fall back on the "time" issue: that there isn't enough of it in the day to do everything they want to do. There is often a large measure of truth to such assertions, but there is virtually no one who doesn't watch an hour of television, spend an hour on social media, or pass an hour away surfing the Internet. That hour could be used for creating.

If a would-be creative doesn't want to trade that hour of TV for an hour of creating, not wanting to trade is the issue. Maybe they're too tired and can only manage to watch television. Then being too tired is the issue. Maybe they've spent their brain cells on the day job. Then spending brain cells is the issue. Maybe their mate makes a face when they try to head for the studio. Then their relationship is the issue. In none of these instances is time really the issue.

When a client has pressing time issues, those issues are both real and also not the whole story. Few people don't have an hour a day available for creating. That hour exists and might be used. At the same time, many people have *only* an hour available, which isn't much and is hard to use when what you want to do is relax, unwind, and not think about things. The absolute best solution to this poignant dilemma is to try to institute a morning creativity practice before your "real day" begins. This isn't the only answer or a complete answer, but it is a solid answer.

When a client has a day job or other time-eating and time-draining responsibilities, I first acknowledge that reality and then say, "That means you will have to create first thing each morning, before you go off to work, because trying to do so when you get home is too darn difficult, given that most of our brain cells are gone by that point." I try to sell all clients on creating first thing each day, because that is the single most important change they can make in the movement from not creating to creating. If a client responds (as many will), "I'm not a morning person" or "That would mean I would have to get up at five in the morning" or "That's when I meditate," my response is "What is your creative life worth?"

This cold-water approach helps resistant creatives move from fantasizing about creating to actually creating. All creatives have a rich fantasy life; that is one of their defining features. This is wonderful—and also a problem. Winning the Nobel Prize in your imagination is not the same as actually winning it. Fantasizing about success is not the same as trying, failing, picking yourself up, trying again, failing again, trying harder, and so on.

Fantasy is a great thing and it is also one of a creative person's prime defenses, since they can "get what they want" in their imagination and are therefore less motivated to try to get it in real life. You can avoid this wrong kind of fantasizing by instituting a morning creativity practice.

There are three important reasons for instituting a morning creativity practice. The first is the obvious one: you'd be getting a lot of creative work done. Even if only a percentage of what you did pleased you, by virtue of working regularly, you'd start to create a body of work. A second reason is you'd get to make use of your "sleep thinking"— you'd benefit from your brain's ability to create and problem-solve while you sleep. Third, you'd have the experience of making meaning on that day. And even if the rest of the day turned out to be half-meaningless, you'd be less likely to despair. By creating first thing in the morning, you would build up "meaning capital" each day.

Of course, managing to institute a morning creativity practice, which is a wonderful thing, does not change the fact that a daily grind is a real grind. It is emotionally, existentially, and physically wearing to have to spend a majority of your waking hours getting to a job that means nothing in particular to you, working, and then getting home while trying to really leave that job behind you, the residue of it trailing along after you. We paste on a smile, try to surrender to the fact that we do not have a trust fund or a partner who is making enough for us to live on, but we aren't really well. How could we be? We are being robbed, pure and simple, of opportunity and energy. And we know it.

How can we best survive this daily grind? We must begin any such investigation with the headline that **there is no perfect answer.** The best answer is to make such deep peace with our situation that it isn't experienced as painful, and, no doubt, some enlightened beings are equal to that feat. Most of us, however, can't quite rise to that lofty place. To get our creating done when we can and to smile about the rest of life, whatever the rest of life brings us, are wonderfully high-bar goals to aspire to. And while we are aspiring to those high-bar goals, we should try the following:

1. **Produce work that is wanted.** It would be lovely if your creative efforts paid the bills. The odds against that are long, but some creatives do live by creating. Most who do must meet the strict demands of the marketplace, producing work that is wanted, that is commercial, while embracing all the marketing and promoting duties that come with selling. There is nothing particularly romantic about having to write the ninth cozy mystery in your cozy mystery series and then having to hawk it to your audience. But if your cozy mystery series is paying the bills, then writing it and selling it is a more palatable option than going off to wait tables.

2.  **Get great at cobbling.** Maybe you can't live by creating alone, but perhaps you can cobble together a living while working independently. And if cobbling doesn't take up every minute of your life, it might prove a rather ideal solution. What might that look like? Maybe live painting classes, online painting classes, mentoring young painters, and the sale of your own paintings together make a living. Maybe this includes running painting retreats in Mexico and the south of France. Maybe it includes the marketing and selling of low-cost spin-off items, like a line of prints or greeting cards. This cobbling would amount to a great deal of work, but it might suit you and spare the need for a day job.

3.  **Day job or second career?** Which is better for you? A "day job" or a "second career," in addition to your creative career? Would the daily grind prove easier if you were a therapist, lawyer, book editor, accountant, or life coach than if you were walking dogs, waiting tables, or delivering packages? The answer isn't a completely obvious "Yes!" That second career

would itself likely prove taxing, draining, and only half-meaningful; nor would there be any rock-solid guarantee of a living wage. Nevertheless, it is a real question to consider. If you conclude that the daily grind would indeed prove easier if you possessed a second career, then you have plotting and planning to do.

4. **Make small changes.** There are, no doubt, many small but not insignificant changes that you might make to your daily routine and your basic attitude. You might create during lunch rather than check e-mails or surf the Net. You might engage in a morning life-purpose check-in, to remind yourself of your intentions and to get clear about how and when you will get to your life purposes that day. You might practice anxiety management, to better deal both with your day job and creative process. You might create ceremonies of peace, hope, and serenity and practice them at work and home. These are all things to try.

You might work on thinking thoughts that serve you. For instance, "I can create" on the commute home rather than "This is hell" or

"I am so tired and miserable." You might try to make positive changes at work, by saying something that needs to be said, negotiating different or fewer hours, ventilating and defusing a long-standing disagreement. Maybe there is a better day job to find, a new effort to be made to "leave work at work," a home-based money-making business to begin that might lead to financial freedom.

One or more of the above tips may make a difference, and several together may make a *huge* difference. There are, of course, many other things to try. Make your own list of possibilities. If something seems worth pursuing, see if you can get to it sooner rather than later. You can't sweep that daily grind away with one grand gesture, but there are things to try.

## Day Job Rage

Paul Gauguin, like most artists forced to work a day job, hated it, ran off to Tahiti to paint, and offered up the following mocking advice in his journal: "Why work? The gods are there to lavish upon the faithful the good gifts of nature."

An artist clear on how little chance she has to run off to Tahiti would happily throw a coconut at Paul's head if he weren't already dead and buried. Still, toiling away at her day job, an artist can't help but wonder, "Is this really the way I should be living?" Such was the question that my painter client Patricia couldn't get off her mind, saddled as she was with a forty-hour-a-week day job.

That day job, working in a Manhattan restaurant, hadn't seemed so terrible when she was in her twenties. Now that she'd turned thirty, it had become unbearable. She knew she was lucky: the restaurant hadn't closed, as so many others had; meals there were expensive, which meant that her tips were large; and her boss was no angel but no monster either. She knew that as day jobs went, hers was pretty excellent. But it was unbearable—and how little painting she was getting done!

To begin with, we could not come up with any great answers. Could she perhaps take a year off and live on parental money and do a lot of painting? No, her parents hated her decision to be an artist and absolutely would not support her; nor could she see herself asking them for money. Might another day job suit her better? No, this one was great, as day jobs went. Maybe she should train in a career and become a therapist, a life coach, or some other professional? No, how long that would take and how far that would take her from painting! Maybe, like in a romantic fantasy movie, she could snare a rich man who would support her. No, neither was she very likely to stand for that!

What then? Waste money on lottery tickets? Drink a lot and drown her sorrows? We finally agreed on a short-term six-month plan, which focused on her getting much more painting done and taking the demands of being a professional artist much more seriously. Did creating this plan allow her to give up her day job? No, of course not. It did, however, provide her with a glimmer of hope.

As might have been expected, the first month of the plan proved rocky. We had agreed that she would check in via e-mail every day, and she missed many days. Often on the days when she did check in, her message amounted to "didn't paint today." But the second month was better, and by the third month she was painting quite a bit, three and sometimes four times a week. Then she stopped abruptly.

We talked. A new issue had arisen. It turned out that her father, who hated the choice she had made to become a painter, was himself a painter and a pretty successful one. It is always a red flag when a client informs me that a close relative creates. It is one sort of red flag if that relative had little success and communicated angst and failure. It is another sort of red flag if that relative, in fact, had success.

When that relative is your father, a creature whose authority and shadow powerfully affect you and everyone in the family, there are bound to be consequences.

Her father, it turned out, was a rather successful landscape painter of the old school, one who took pride in his ability to render the natural world. He was represented by several galleries, knew his collectors by name, had an established auction price, and played the marketplace game very well. Patricia couldn't quite tell if she respected her father's work or found it clichéd and boring—or both. She was sure, however, that something about their relationship was stifling her and paralyzing her and had suddenly caused her to stop painting . . . again.

It was hard to identify the exact problem. He had never formally critiqued or rudely criticized her paintings. But when he looked at them, which happened very rarely, he would wear a certain smile that Patricia took to mean he found them wanting. Perhaps most significantly, he had never introduced her to his contacts in the art world, of whom he had many, even when she felt she had produced enough good work for a show. She had asked him once if he would help; he refused, citing what she thought was the lame, mean-spirited excuse that he didn't want her to "have it too easy." She never asked him again.

She couldn't figure it out, and we couldn't figure it out. She wondered if he was envious of her, if he feared she would outshine him, if he hated her abstractions, or if something very different was going on. She just couldn't tell. She'd journaled about it, been in therapy about it, obsessed about it, pledged not to think about it, and then went right back to thinking about it. Not a day went by that she didn't wonder "What was up?" with her father, with whom she spoke rarely. And, slowly but surely, not a day went by that she didn't forego painting, until her recent resumption.

"Well, you had gotten back to painting," I said, "which was wonderful. We can't let this mysterious problem derail you. What's our best tactic, do you think?"

She thought about that. "Well, if he were to die, I would begin painting immediately."

"All right. But you aren't going to wait for that, are you?"

"No." A light bulb clicked on. "I know what I want to do. I want to do a series of abstracted—that's not it, exactly—maybe defaced versions of his landscapes. That's exciting to me!"

I wondered. "Are you sure? You've been loving your subject matter."

"I can get back to that. This is important. I think it would be part homage, part response, and part revenge. Then, you know what? I would approach one of his galleries and suggest a joint show! That would be something. I bet they'd go for it! This is exactly what I want to do."

I had to smile. "Very mysterious, this relationship."

"And this is the perfect continuation of that mystery."

The next month was hard. She began her new series of paintings and at the same time tackled the business side of painting. She started to look with a realistic eye at what seemed to be working for artists who were succeeding financially. That taxed her! But by the end of the month, she had some ideas as to what she might try to build her brand and become better known, ideas connected to her "mysterious father-daughter enterprise." She was managing to paint, to look at business matters, to get to work, and to deal with daily grind. . . . But it all felt very effortful, tumultuous, and tenuous.

Then she stopped painting again.

"It's rage," she said at our next session.

Her situation enraged her. It enraged her that she had to work that day job. It enraged her that customers spent 150 dollars a person for a meal at the restaurant where she worked. It enraged her that she had so many finished paintings accumulated with nothing to do with them. The commodification of art enraged her. What she saw in galleries enraged her. The world enraged her.

But her rage ran deeper and wider even than all that. She hated the way her parents wrote her off and dismissed as indulgent and ridiculous her desire to be a painter, even though her father painted! She hated how she had been bullied in childhood and made to feel scared by her father's rages and tantrums. She hated with a burning hatred the world's cavalier injustices, the millions upon millions of shameless outrages perpetrated daily.

I tried to formulate the question on my mind. "How would you describe your relationship to that rage? Are you 'for it' or 'against it'?"

She thought about it. Then, after a long while, she said, "I'm attached to it."

That was a big-deal insight.

"And do you want to stay attached to it?"

"I'm not sure."

"Tell me the pros and cons of staying attached to your rage."

"I have a very refined sense of fairness and justice. Therefore, *not* noticing injustice and unfairness wouldn't sit right. I'd be lying somehow."

"But we aren't talking about noticing. We're talking about raging."

"That's true. I could truthfully see without also getting enraged. Could I? Could I truthfully see without getting enraged?"

"What if it were for the sake of painting? What if you said to yourself, 'My rage kills my ability to paint'? Wouldn't that make rage a much less attractive attachment?"

She thought about that. "I think it would."

"And does that feel true, that your rage *is* killing your ability to paint?"

"Yes."

That conversation proved pivotal. It took time, but Patricia formed the intention to let go of her rage. She created the mantra "Inner peace and life purpose" and began to use it. As a result—and as a continuation of the mysterious relationship between her father and her—she stopped painting defaced replicas of his landscapes and then returned to it.

"But without the underlying rage," she said to me. "At least, without so much of the underlying rage. Now it interests me aesthetically and artistically. Something about it is truly fascinating to me."

The daily grind remained the daily grind for Patricia. But she learned that unexplored feelings made matters much worse. She continued painting, and a gallery accepted two of her "defaced landscapes," and then one of them sold for its asking price. She had the sense that a slight ripple effect had begun. She also knew she was dreading getting something from her father—an e-mail, a phone call, or pregnant silence, which would be worse than hearing from him—and she was steeling herself for that. At the same time, she found herself smiling. Part of her couldn't wait for his response, which never came. She had rather expected that, and because she had prepared herself for such an outcome, she was able to continue painting even though her relationship with her father was anything but resolved.

Making enough money to be able to live is a painful part of virtually every creative individual's personal story. Some opt for second careers, which then consume them. Others become dependent on loved ones (whom they may or may not love). Others struggle with poor-paying, demeaning day jobs. Others collect skills and degrees, learn coaching or get certificates in massage therapy and yoga, which then do not quite come together into a viable whole. Others (and this is many a creative's ongoing nightmare) end up homeless and down-and-out. A few "make it" in their art discipline and then discover a whole new world of challenge and grind.

How can you heal the emotional pain of having to struggle so hard just to make ends meet if maintaining a day job remains an ongoing reality for you? One way is to maintain hope that you may one day be able to give up your day job. To maintain that hope, you need to create a plan that strikes you as plausible. At this moment, you may have no idea what such a plan ought to include. That is your work then: learning for yourself what such a plausible business plan might look like. I hope you can face this task and master it. By creating a smart business plan, by dealing with any emotional blocks that may be making matters worse, and by getting clear on which might serve you better (a day job or a second career), you give yourself the best chance possible of thriving as a working artist.

# Chapter 9

## REDUCING INTERNAL DRAMAS

Some of the difficulties that creatives and would-be creatives face are rather self-inflicted. One sort of self-inflicted difficulty is magnifying real difficulties and turning rocky hills into icy mountains. A second self-inflicted difficulty is getting attached, even addicted, to drama, to the extent that our lives end up revolving around inner histrionics and prevent us from living our life purposes.

Many creatives and would-be creatives are terribly attracted to drama, often without even knowing it. What does this attraction look like? Here are four typical self-inflicted dramas that I regularly encounter when I coach creative and performing artists.

1. **You're a writer.** Someone you know says she'll be happy to read your completed manuscript. You send it to her. She replies she is, in fact,

too busy to read it. From this relatively trivial event, you create the most intense, dramatic, exclamation-point-littered story about betrayal, humiliation, failure, and the essential cruelty of the universe. Why would a writer do that and derail herself for six months, a year, or forever? Why? Chalk it up to our human penchant for careless overdramatizing.

2. **You're a painter.** You've finished new paintings, and you're not sure what to charge for them. You have good reasons for charging what you usually charge, for increasing your prices, and for charging almost any amount under the sun, from next to nothing to an outlandish amount, given the extraordinary range of prices attached to paintings. Rather than make a reasoned choice, you turn this everyday difficulty into dramatic paralysis and stop selling and painting. You throw up your hands and descend into despair. All because you couldn't price your paintings!

3. **You're a singer/songwriter.** You've written new songs and want to record them. But you're not sure which ones to record. This one sounds

nicely commercial, but is it too commercial? This one is very arty, but is it too quiet? This one is excellent and requires an accompanist, but who's available? This one is catchy, but doesn't it vaguely sound like somebody else's song? You stew about this, and keep raising the heat under the pot until the stew is boiling. Should it be this song, that song, or the other song? This song, that song, or the other song? THIS SONG, THAT SONG, OR THE OTHER SONG? Finally, the dramatic explosion arrives and you table your project indefinitely.

4. **You're an actor.** Your current headshots have you with short hair, but you think you look better with long hair. So you schedule an expensive photo shoot. The day goes poorly, in part because you're not thrilled by the way you look, in part because the photographer doesn't seem sympathetic to your requests. You get the results, and not one picture thrills you. Some are serviceable, but is serviceable good enough? You throw an internal fit about wasting all that money, about having no headshots that you like, and about the absurdity of the life you're

leading. As a result, you avoid auditioning for the rest of the year because a photo shoot went poorly.

This isn't to say that you *look* dramatic or histrionic. You may not look like much of a drama queen to the world. Indeed, you may look rather mild-mannered and sedate. You may reply calmly when addressed, measure your words, run errands without making a fuss, and appear relatively angst-free. Yet there in that room which is your mind, you may be playing out so many dramas that it's fair to say you're addicted to drama. *There* is where the drama occurs.

Something happens when you enter the room that is your mind. There, the moment you arrive, you are handed permission from yourself to throw a fit, upset all the furniture, and act as if your world has crashed into a million pieces. An engraved invitation was waiting, and you accepted it. Why? Well, life felt a little boring and you craved excitement, even of this unfortunate kind. Maybe this precipitating event was the straw that broke your back. Maybe you're furious about something else, and this was a convenient trigger. Who can say? Whatever the reason for accepting it, you did. Internally, you begin yelling and shrieking.

Since this invitation may be regularly waiting for you, you need to prepare yourself for it. First, pin a sign on the door to the room that is your mind: "No drama queen allowed!" Second, enter that room very carefully, watching out for such invitations. If an invitation is waiting, thrust at you on a silver tray by a butler in livery, shake your head and murmur, "Ah no, you've mistaken me for a diva." Then make sure to stay alert as you move about. Drama may be lurking behind the armoire or under the cushion of your easy chair, waiting to pounce.

Part of us really does crave that drama. I suspect that craving connects to the trickster part of our nature. The trickster figure appears in the oral traditions and shared myths of virtually every indigenous culture. People everywhere have identified this part of our nature. Let's foul the well water. Let's sleep with our neighbor's wife. Let's steal those chickens. Let's do worse. Let's plunder. Let's turn whole communities against one another. Let's make a giant mess of everyone's life. Let's be a trickster!

Where do those sly, nasty, horrible impulses come from that inhabit everyone and that, in modern times, we so often turn against ourselves, self-inflicting wounds, and sabotaging our best efforts? Why do we start the day moral, compassionate, and upright, and somewhere around noon turn into a coyote, ravenous for mischief? No one really knows. The important thing is to recognize this aspect of our personality and to have a conversation with our personal trickster where we announce, in that voice that we use when we really mean something, that we are on to its tricks, that it isn't the least bit amusing, and that we really don't appreciate it.

It seems that a trickster self is usually self-mischievous. Few dancers kneecap other dancers; few writers loot their neighbors' pantries; few singers dream up ways of bringing down laryngitis on their rivals. Modern folks, prevented by conscience from wreaking havoc on others, turn their trickster nature against themselves, mischievously making themselves miserable. They trick themselves into not attending a perfect audition opportunity, tricks herself into not making use of a great marketplace contact, into not replying to a literary agent in a timely fashion. And then they scream bloody murder!

All internal hell breaks loose. We begin shouting, "The world has offended me!" as if "the world" had done something. If we were monarchs, we'd lop off heads, any heads. Not being royalty, we transform that outrage that we ourselves created into further self-sabotage and paralysis. Wouldn't it be ever so much better to banish the trickster and to not play out that mischief and subsequent drama? Put up little signs everywhere: "Trickster forbidden!" and "No dramas, please." Maybe that will make our room a little less exciting, but isn't that the wrong kind of excitement anyway?

What happens when we allow ourselves all these internal dramas? One consequence is we do not give ourselves the chance to come up with answers to our own pressing questions. Something comes up, and we really need an answer. Our mates receive a job offer to work on the other side of the world. Will we accompany them? You have a medical condition that might be treated in any one of three ways. Which treatment will you choose? At such times, do you settle down in the room that is your mind and think calmly? Or do you visit a dramatic environment and grab the first handy answer? "No, I'm not going!" you shout. "No, no chemo for me!" Do you pounce on the first thought waiting for you? And given that you haven't done any real thinking, *Where did that thought even come from?*

When you create internal dramas, you rarely get to second or third answers. You just grab the first answer already waiting there. If an "answer" awaits us as we walk in the door, if an analysis or train of thought or sponta-neous reaction *has already taken place* before we even enter the room that is our mind, doesn't that enslave us to the murky doings of our unconscious and to the straitjacket of our formed personality? And mustn't mastery of ourselves include an awareness that we will meet already-formed answers as soon as we enter that room, and that as powerful and influential as those first answers may feel, they must not be considered our final answer?

Since an automatic answer is likely to be waiting for you in that tumultuous environment and since you are programmed to accept it, you will need to have a chat with yourself when you enter that room. It might sound like this: "I didn't arrive at this answer. It was waiting for me. Since it was already waiting for me, it, no doubt, reflects thoughts and feelings I'm having. But maybe it arose out of anxiety, fear, rage, or who knows what. Since it was waiting for me, that makes it too easy an answer. Instead of reflectively accepting it, I will think. If, upon reflection, I come to the same answer, then I'll trust it more. And if I come to a different answer, well, thank goodness I checked!"

A corollary useful habit to acquire, in addition to not creating unnecessary internal dramas, is to not magnify difficulties. We cause our own distress if we magnify the difficulty of our tasks. Our tasks are already real; there is no need to magnify them. Our language should not be allowed to turn hills into mountains. If we regularly exclaim to ourselves, "That was the worst thing that could have happened!" or "I can't possibly recover from that rejection!" or "Now I really have no chance!" we've made creating and living the creative life all that much harder. Refusing to add incendiary language to our everyday self-talk is a vital habit to cultivate.

Often, we string many prospective difficulties together and by so doing completely exhaust and demoralize ourselves before we've even started. If, as a painter, I say, "Let me call that gallery," I have added no unnecessary distress to an already charged task. If, however, I find myself saying, "Let me call that gallery, but where did I put that number, and I'll probably only get voicemail, and what will I say then, but what if I get a person, what would I say *then*, and I'm not sure I really want that gallery, but if I don't get it I won't be represented anywhere, and that means I will have no career whatsoever," I have worked myself into a lather and made it almost certain that I won't call. If I do manage to call, which is highly unlikely, I'll handle it poorly, having agitated myself so much.

Why do we magnify our difficulties? We magnify them for all sorts of understandable reasons. Maybe our tasks feel that hard. Maybe it pleases us to see ourselves burdened by the sorts of challenges that only a warrior hero could possibly meet. Then, when and if we manage to handle such "huge" issues, we boost our ego. Maybe there is an emotional payoff to feeling ourselves victimized, beleaguered, or put-upon. Maybe life feels boring, and we crave the dramas we create when we pour fuel on small fires. These are common, completely human reasons for engaging in a practice that fails to serve us.

Begin to practice the habit of not magnifying difficulties. You do not need to shrink them and act as if they do not exist. Just don't magnify them. Imagine possessing a mag-nifying glass that does not magnify but simply allows you to see what is there. Imagine how an ant would look through that sort of nonmagnifying glass. It would look like an ant, not like a giant ant out of a horror movie. Imagine how an everyday task would look. Get in the habit of using this nonmagnifying glass. Even if there is an emotional payoff to turning ordinary difficulties into huge internal dramas, the downside is significantly greater.

Often, we create these dramas and magnify these difficulties as a defense against recognizing what is really going on or noticing the big changes that we need to make. Maybe you don't want to acknowledge that you haven't made any real progress on your novel in years. Maybe you don't want to see all that painting inventory piling up. Maybe it's changing your day job and getting away from your traumatizing boss, or separating from your mate, or curtailing your drinking. This thing that you are defending yourself against knowing feels huge, dangerous, and consequential, that you can't get anywhere near allowing it into conscious awareness. You have the thought "I hate my boss!", bite your lip, create an internal drama, and drown out that thought with self-inflicted mayhem and noise.

A wonderful habit to learn is to tolerate such thoughts for more than a split second. Just practice tolerating "I haven't been making progress on my novel" or "I need a new day job." Notice how you are barraged by feelings the instant you think that thought. Notice how you want to flee, by creating a huge internal drama. Implore yourself to stay with the precipitating thought. That's the whole goal: to stay with it, rather than fleeing from it or drowning it out.

Bring up a thought that you don't want to think. That alone may feel horribly hard. Now, try to tolerate it. In order to make the changes you need to make in life, the first step is tolerating thoughts. Don't worry about "doing anything" with the feelings that flood you as you stay with that difficult thought. You don't have to dispute them, answer them, handle them, accept them, or anything at all. You just have to survive them. You only have to tolerate them. Surviving them and tolerating them will make it easier for you to really "be with" a difficult thought the next time one arises.

The habit of tolerating a difficult thought and tolerating the feelings that come flooding in on the heels of it begins to create calmness and an opening for reasoned thinking, needed change, and invaluable hope. You will begin to see that you can survive thinking difficult thoughts, and decisions and action steps are likely to come next. Whether or not they do come each and every time, tolerating a difficult thought is nevertheless a brilliant habit to learn. Begin to visualize the room that is your mind as a safe haven.

## I Must Dance or Die

I was looking for a venue for a deep-writing workshop in Rome and landed on a brilliant location, the University of Washington's Rome Center, right at a corner of the Piazza Campo de' Fiori. How marvelous to teach in a sunlit room with a grand view of the city and how marvelous to visit with the group after class at one or another of the cafés at our doorstep.

I took the opportunity to visit with a client of mine, an American dancer in her late thirties who, fluent in Italian as well as English, was working as a medical secretary while recovering from injuries. She had been dancing in Europe with a rather well-known company but had gotten laid up, and now she felt hopeless, fearing she might never dance again professionally.

I'd rented a place near the Vatican, high up a steep hill in a quiet location, and because she lived in that neighborhood, too, we met at a café on the nontouristy shopping street called Via Cola Di Rienzo. We'd talked a few times before via Skype, and I knew her story from the e-mail responses she'd provided to my initial questions. This was the first time we were meeting in person, and after the usual pleasantries she said, "If I can't dance, I have no reason to live."

This dramatic thought, which, of course, was not serving her at all, had to be disputed by me, but ever so carefully and diplomatically.

I nodded. "But you do have other loves?" I wondered.

"I have other likes," she replied. "I have only one love."

"What are some of those likes?" I pursued.

"I like cooking. I like the memoir I'm writing. Or, rather, I like it some of the time. I like Europe. You know, likes like those."

I nodded again. "And something like the writing? It couldn't rise to the level of love?"

"I don't know."

I didn't press. We sat quietly. Passersby hurried up and down the busy street.

"As to dancing professionally," I said, "what happens in your forties, fifties, sixties, seventies, eighties, nineties?"

"What do you mean?"

"You intend to dance professionally then?"

She laughed mirthlessly. "No, I intend to kill myself. I want to dance professionally for as long as I can and then that's that."

She turned away and watched the street. Every second person was attacking a huge ice cream cone, scooped at the famous ice creamery a few doors down from us. Some cones sported three scoops, which defied decorum and engineering. She spent a long time watching the street.

"I will kill myself," she said finally. "I mean it. I've tried it before, half-heartedly, but the next time it won't be half-hearted."

Now it was my turn to look out. It was a beautiful day in Rome, but it was impossible for my client to enjoy it. All she could do was obsess about the horror of not dancing. Fueling that obsessive thought were all sort of traumas, grievances, and dramas. I'd previously learned that her parents were cruel and unsupportive, that she'd had a long, disastrous affair with a married well-known choreographer and then another, that she was at that point in her life where she was ratifying the decision she had made long ago not to have children, and that her dance injuries were not healing properly. All of that perpetuated the drama that without dance life was not worth living.

She hated her job as a medical secretary. The men of Rome were obnoxious. The air quality was terrible. The tourists were impossible. The government was fascist. It wasn't much better at home in the United States. Traveling was getting harder all the time: the airports, the canceled flights. Plus, her boss gave her so little vacation that she couldn't travel much anywhere. And with her healing going slowly, traveling was hardly enjoyable anyway. More to fuel the drama of not dancing!

I knew what answers couldn't possibly work. It wouldn't work to inquire whether she could dance "for fun." She would make a face at that and internally announce I didn't understand her at all. It wouldn't work to put other possible life-purpose choices on the table, like service or activism. She would only nod at those and agree they were perfectly worthy for *someone*, but they weren't dance. "I was put on this earth to dance," she would almost surely say. And that would be that.

We sat quietly. After a while, I said, "You know, you will have to change your mind."

"About what?"

"That dancing is the only thing that can matter."

"I'll never change my mind about that."

But she did. First, she made another effort to dance professionally. But her body didn't hold up well, nor did her spirits. We continued working together, and I continued carefully exploring whether she might be able to invest in new life purposes. At the same time, I continued trying to help her reduce her internal dramas.

Then, in a Skype session, she said, "I've been chatting with the patients who come in to our medical office. I can see that the ones who talk the most dramatically and shrilly about their medical problems also do the most poorly. I think I'm beginning to see what you've been saying." She couldn't help but smile at her observation.

This led to a conclusion neither of us could have foreseen: she commenced writing a nonfiction book for medical patients, which she tentatively called *Less Drama, More Healing*. I had to smile. She is working on that book and looking for a dance class that she might take "just for fun."

# Chapter 10

## MEETING THE MARKETPLACE

Most creatives are disinclined to deal with the marketplace. They may fantasize about success but at the same time not feel equal to dealing with literary agents, editors, gallery owners, musical venue owners, and potential independent film donors. This disinclination not only prevents them from having the career they want, but ultimately it limits their ability to unleash their creative potential. How easy will it prove to write your next novel if your first several novels are languishing away in computer files? Not very easy at all.

There are scores of reasons why a creative might be disinclined to deal with the marketplace. Let's look at a sampling and what you can do in each instance:

1. **Finding that anxiety gets in the way.**
   Strategy: Acquire an anxiety management tool or two. Few people consciously practice anx-

iety management. Every artist should. The techniques available to you include breathing exercises (one deep cleansing breath can work wonders), brief meditations, guided visualizations (where, for example, you picture yourself relaxed and calm), discharge techniques (for example, getting your pent-up anxiety released through "silent screaming"), personality work (for instance, practicing acting "as if" you feel confident), and cognitive restructuring (that is, changing the things you say to yourself and thereby reducing your experience of anxiety).

2. **Not knowing what to say.** Strategy: First, practice what you intend to say. You should be able to say about your painting, "This is one of a series of paintings I'm doing that emphasizes the horizontal element in landscape." It doesn't matter if that is what you are "really" doing in your painting, because what you are really doing is beyond language. You are simply providing yourself with something better to do than grunt, mutter, ramble, and fumble.

Second (and in seeming contradiction to the first), do not feel that you need to have anything to say. Feel free to reply to a query about your painting's meaning with a cheerful "Lord, if I know!" Relax. At the same time, be prepared with good answers.

3.  **Feeling one-down or one-up to people who hold the power and purse strings.** Strategy: inner work on feeling equal. Although it is not easy to do, it is possible to get a grip on your mind and rethink the way you hold marketplace players, reminding yourself that your goal is to feel neither inferior nor superior to them, but as if you and they were in the art-buying-and-selling enterprise together. If your tendency is to feel superior, remind yourself, "No smirking!" If your tendency is to feel inferior, remind yourself, "Backbone, please!"

    Our typical reaction to power is a version of the fight-or-flight syndrome: we want to strike first, or we want to run and hide. The less you hold these interactions as threatening, the less your fight-or-flight reflex will kick in and the more equal you'll manage to feel.

4.  **Not enjoying selling yourself.** Strategy: First, begin to enjoy selling yourself! That is what

you are doing, so enjoy it. Have nice things to say about yourself, couched beautifully so that you don't come off as too arrogant or grandiose. Drop well-crafted nuggets about your successes and accomplishments. Be your own best friend and advocate. Who else will be?

Second, disidentify from each of your products. You are not your painting, and you do not have to die a little death if your painting is not wanted by this or that person. You can and should announce its merits and advocate for its worth without, however, attaching to the outcome of each interaction. This can sound like "I truly enjoyed painting this juxtaposition of floating roses on a traditional landscape background. I think it worked well." Smile, and cherish no expectations.

5. **Dealing with people who dismiss you or who are difficult.** Strategy: simple professionalism. Try not to burn bridges. Try not to act out. Try not to react much at all. If the person who dismisses you is cruel and insulting, protect yourself from that person but also decide whether it is worth your while to respond and

get embroiled in a drama. That drama could cost you sleepless nights and days missed in the studio. If the dismissal is an everyday rejection, one of the zillions we face because we have chosen to create, merely shrug and practice your "rejection management skills," which might or might not include a lot of chocolate.

6. **Not feeling up to asking.** Strategy: We will have a whole chapter on this coming up. Often, we are unwilling to ask—for a gallery show, space in a crafts shop, the name and e-mail address of somebody it would be good for us to contact, a favor from a friend who knows somebody we ought to get to know—out of anxiety, out of pride, and, in a few cases, because we feel that we ought to be able to reciprocate in some way.

   As to anxiety, management is the key. As to pride, you need to talk yourself down off your high horse by reminding yourself that you, in fact, need lots of help in life. Third, if you feel that you have no way to reciprocate, remind yourself that a favor does not have to be repaid the instant it is granted. Say "thank you" and remember that you owe a good turn.

7. **Not knowing what to do.** Strategy: Accept that the marketplace comes with a large measure of mystery and opaqueness and that trying to fathom what really works and what you ought to try is more like a guessing game than a rational enterprise. That being said, there are reasonable and rational things to do that, while not coming with any guarantees, are better than sitting on your hands and not trying.

   Often you will simply not know what to do. At the very least, you can do research and see if anybody has been successful hawking your sorts of wares. If someone has, there must be something to learn from their efforts. If no one has, you may have to dream up out-of-the-box tactics to have any chance of success. That, then, will prove your job: not only to create but also to create the appetite for what you create and, in effect, create your audience.

8. **Dealing with the daily grind of marketing, promoting, and running a one-person business.** Strategy: We talked about the daily grind of a day job in chapter eight. Then there is the daily grind of running your one-person busi-

ness, which is what your art business is. It is its own grind. You aren't done when you've sold one book, one painting, or one song. You aren't done when you've performed once or made one independent film. All of the chores that came with making that first film, from raising money to scoring it to your liking to entering it into those film festivals in the Balkans, will return for your second film and your third film.

What must you do? Accept this reality. You may fantasize about a sort of "hit moment" that makes you so desirable and popular that all those chores vanish, but not only is that outsized success unlikely, the tasks will continue and even multiply. Accept that you have decided to run a certain one-person business, with expenses, inventory, customer service needs, and all the rest. Maybe—fingers crossed—you will even enjoy that; a number of creatives do. But whether or not you enjoy it, let out a big sigh and accept it. Fighting that reality will exhaust you.

9. **Issues around whether you deserve success, whether your work has any merit or reasons for being, and other shadowy**

**matters.** Strategy: Millions of individuals must heal from trauma and deal with the lifelong negative consequences that rock us and shatter us. Some of those effects, like a loss of self-esteem, increased anxiety, pervasive shame, deep despair, intractable addiction, chronic fatigue, nagging physical ailments, and meaning shortfalls, contribute to our resistance to marketing ourselves and our reluctance to "put ourselves out there."

We heal by growing aware of our truth and dealing with each effect in its own way, say by working a twelve-step program for the addiction while practicing anxiety manage-ment for the anxiety, learning what triggers our painful thoughts and feelings and avoiding those triggers that can be avoided, and in these and many other ways creating and living a complete self-care program. When we do this, we give ourselves our best chance possible of coming out from the shadows and bravely facing the marketplace.

10. **A stubborn desire "not to give in" and not to play "all those marketplace games."**

Strategy: It is individuality that defines a creative person. Smart, sensitive creatives will already know as young children that they can't conform and weren't built that way. Looking around, unable to understand why people are acting so conventionally, starting to feel alienated, out of place, and like a "stranger in a strange land," they find themselves burdened by this pulsing energy: the fierce need to be themselves. This need produces lifelong consequences, including an abiding stubbornness to reject humbug and to make personal sense of the world. This adamancy is likely to result in a stubborn need to reject the "humbug" of sales, an activity they are likely to see as the very essence of conformity.

The mandate to individuality forces creative persons to wonder about life's large questions—pesters them with those questions—and demands that they respond to what they see going on in the universe. It forces them to write a mournful poem, craft a subversive novel, and walk the earth from one end to the other on an unnamable quest. Each of these is an existential response, that is, a response arising from their plaintive, poignant questioning of the world into which nature has dropped them. On top of everything else, nature tells them that they are responsible for looking out for the world—nothing less is expected of them. And instead of this, they are supposed to engage in *sales*?

The strategic answers are, first, to reframe the matter so that "sales" becomes "self-advocacy"; and, second, to remind yourself that your creative life is not a zero-sum game where, if you sell for an hour, that somehow means that you can't create something breathtaking and world-shattering during the next hour. Fighting to retain your individuality ought not to mean fighting tooth-and-nail *against* selling. Somewhere just out of conscious awareness, creatives are hearing not "selling" but "selling out." They are not the same things. Yes, you have to be careful not to sink into the vast morass of unscrupulous business tactics; and that morass is vast. But you must advocate for yourself: that is the bottom line.

One tactic that may help you counter your disinclination to deal with the marketplace is to remind yourself that you do not need to be "the real you" in all of your dealings with the marketplace. You can adopt a public persona that functions better than "the real you" might and that allows you to keep a self-protective distance between you and the world of sales.

Adopting a public persona is a way to practice "doing better" in public than you typically do in private. You might craft a public persona that allows you to exhibit more confidence than you actually feel, be clear when you feel fuzzy, and ask pointed questions that you would avoid asking if you were only having a conversation with yourself. In this sense, your public persona can reflect the changes that you would like to make to upgrade your personality and, in fact, *be* your go-to personality upgrade effort.

Of course, you may be quite happy with who you are "in private" and not see any need for a personality upgrade. Still, you may recognize that your irony doesn't play well in public, that your frankness tends to be received as brusqueness, and that the qualities you take pride in ought to be modulated or moderated in a public setting. In this scenario, you create a strategic public persona that matches "what the world wants" and that allows you to interact effectively with customers, collectors, framers, gallery owners, media representatives, and the other people with whom you should be interacting.

Janet, a painter, explained to me: "Whether by nature or nurture, I am a shy person who prefers to spend her time in the studio and who will do almost anything to avoid marketplace interactions. This way of being suited me better when I was learning my craft, as I really did need to focus on what was going on in the studio. But now that I have an overflowing body of work, I need to step out into the world in ways that I find strange and uncomfortable. I have to make myself do it, and it does not come naturally. I actually have a checklist of the qualities I want to manifest, which I keep by my computer, so that every e-mail I send out is coming from my public persona and not my shy studio personality."

Jack, a sculptor, told me: "I've been in recovery for eight years. Before that, when I was actively drinking, I always led with my temper. I had an attacking style. I would interrupt you, contradict you, fight you over every detail and the smallest perceived grievance, and always get in the last word. I was angry all the time, which was a good thing with respect to the sculptures, as they had a lot of good angry energy to them, but which was not good anywhere else in my life. Over these eight years of recovery, I've cultivated a way of being that is more temperate, centered, and essentially gentle. Actually, I'm really still as hard as nails and people really ought not to cross me. But that part of me is kept under lock and key and almost never appears in public these days."

Creating a public persona is a useful exercise and a smart enterprise. Give some thought to who you want to be in public. Artists' public personas are the measured presentation of those qualities that they have identified will serve them best in the public arena. What qualities would you like to lead with in your public interactions? How would you like to be perceived? What public persona would allow you to advocate for your work most effectively? Build that persona and then outfit it with a full wardrobe. Give it hats, shoes, gloves, and clothes for every occasion. Construct a "you" who can do well in the world.

## The Reluctant Painter

Virtually all of my creative and performing artist clients have troubles with the marketplace, in large measure because the odds of success are tremendously long and because they prefer to make art or to perform rather than to deal with the marketplace.

Marsha was no exception. Like everyone, she came with a past and a personality. Her sister's accidental death at the age of twelve and her family's collapse after that terrible incident robbed Marsha of something: joy; confidence; hope for her own future; something. It also robbed her of her health. She grew sickly. She suffered with chronic earaches. And it made painting, which was the light of her life, painful and difficult. As a result, she produced little—lovely things but only occasional things.

A point came when these occasional things had accumulated. Marsha was by then in her early thirties. She had a friend by the name of Meredith, who had a friend by the name of Valerie. Valerie ran a small, prestigious gallery, and Meredith suggested that Valerie see Marsha's work. A studio visit got arranged. Valerie arrived; Marsha, her ear aching and her nerves raw, awkwardly showed Valerie around—it didn't take that long. Valerie left, and something about that visit and the ensuing silence from Valerie provoked Marsha to come see me.

"How did the visit go?" I asked after we were settled.

"It was pleasant. It went fine."

"What did she say?"

"That she liked my work a lot."

"And?"

"And?"

"Did you ask her if she wanted to give you a show?"

"No. She didn't seem that interested."

"She said that she liked your work a lot. But she didn't seem that interested?"

"Exactly. I sensed that she was being polite. She didn't have much to say about my work as she was looking at it."

"What *did* she say? Besides, that she liked it a lot?"

"Oh, she said this and that. She thought that I had a tremendous color sense, that I had a unique perspective, things like that."

"And that sounded like mere politeness?"

"Well, she didn't say that she loved anything! And she didn't . . . I don't know . . . have a lot to say."

I wished I could smile.

"What would you have said to van Gogh about *Starry Night*?" I asked after a moment.

Marsha shrugged. "I don't know. That I loved it."

"And? What else?"

"I don't know. Maybe nothing."

"Not 'What an interesting way to paint stars'?"

"God, no!"

"Not 'How much you've crammed into such a small canvas!'?"

"No!"

"And since you would have stood there mute or nearly mute, he should have taken that to mean you were just being polite when you said that you loved it?"

She frowned.

"Maybe she really liked my work," she said after a long moment.

"So you'll get in touch with her?"

Marsha closed right down. "Well . . . "

"Yes?"

"My paintings are of very different sizes. They wouldn't make for a coherent show."

"So you're mind-reading again?"

"Mind-reading? No . . . I know how shows work."

"Is that right? There's a show at the Modern." I mentioned the name of a well-known artist. "You've seen it?"

"Yes."

"What are the sizes of the paintings in that show?"

Marsha thought about that. "Every size under the sun. Miniatures. Huge things."

"And so?"

"She's famous. She can get away with different sizes."

"I see. She started out famous?"

"No."

"And all of her early works were of one size?"

"No. I'm sure they weren't."

"So you'll get in touch with Valerie?"

She shut down further. "I've taken too long to get back to her," she said. "I missed that train."

"And you know that how?"

"Just intuition. I'm extremely intuitive."

"How long has it been?"

"A month. Almost two."

"Do you want a show?"

This question stopped her for a moment. Then she said, "Maybe I don't." It was a very breezy answer. "I'm not sure her gallery is really right for me. I should go check it out again. Plus, it's so expensive to frame things. She didn't say who would have to pay for the framing. I'm sure it would have to be me. I don't know if I want to pay for the framing and then not sell anything and get more depressed. So, no, probably not. I don't want a show at her gallery."

I nodded. "I see. But similar issues would arise with any gallery? So you don't want a show at any gallery?"

She thought about that. Suddenly, she brightened. "Yes, I think that's right! I think that I don't actually want a gallery show. I think I want something different—a more human way to show my work. Maybe a sort of collective effort. I should start a group gallery in an alternative space. But I don't have the strength for that. So I would have to find a group that already exists. But the ones that already exist are cliquish, and I don't do that well with groups. . . . "

We continued in this vein until the end of the session. I plugged away at wondering out loud how it could be a bad thing to contact Valerie and secure a show at her gallery.

Marsha countered each suggestion with her reasons as to why such a show was either a bad idea or a complete impossibility. At the end of the session she gave a small, wry smile, as if to say, "I'm really difficult, aren't I?" Or maybe her smile meant, "I think I won. But what a victory!"

Had we made any progress? Marsha was certainly not a changed person. Still, because we had been talking about the right things, I would have bet that a seed had been planted. If we'd been witness to her inner dialogue, I'm sure we would have overheard a conversation between her frightened, irritable, stubbornly negative everyday voice and that other voice, the one that guided the painting, appreciated life, and would have loved a little success. How would that conversation have ended? Probably not with her picking up the phone and calling Valerie. I would have set the odds at her making that call at four-to-one against, five-to-one against, or more. But bigger odds are an improvement over being scratched from the race entirely.

Two months later I got an e-mail from Marsha setting up another appointment. A week after that we met on Skype.

"I contacted Valerie," she said. "She'd like to give me a show."

"That's great!"

"But I have a lot of concerns, so I haven't said *yes*."

"But you haven't said *no*?" I held my breath.

"No. I said *maybe*."

"Okay," I said. "We can go through your concerns one by one. But first I have to ask you: what's going on?"

Her face crumpled. "I don't know. I feel like fleeing the country."

We talked. Wherever the conversation took us, I never took my eye off my crystal-clear goal: to help Marsha say *yes* to Valerie. We tackled what Marsha felt were certain suspect clauses in the gallery contract. We tackled what felt to Marsha like Valerie's unseemly pressure on her to help promote the show. We tackled what felt to Marsha like Valerie's bossiness and inability to quite hear what she was saying. I walked on eggshells, trying to say nothing that might suggest the least bit that the bottom line ought to be a *no*.

"These are all manageable," I said. "Nothing huge here!"

"You think?"

"I do."

She remained skeptical, because her reluctance had little if anything to do with her stated concerns. Her real concerns resided somewhere else, in a place we hadn't quite accessed yet.

"I don't know," she said as we approached the end of the session. "I'm on the fence."

"I hope you agree to the show," I said.

"We'll see."

What do you think? Want to cast your vote? Did Marsha agree to the show or not? She did. She explained to me in an e-mail, "I'm not sure what my reluctance is all about. I do feel reluctant. But I had a dream, and in that dream I saw a young woman looking at one of my paintings in a gallery and being moved by it. I can't have that without my paintings actually being in a gallery, can I? Is this the right gallery? Is this the right moment? I don't know. But I'm going to say *yes*. Yes to the gallery and yes to something else that I can't quite name."

It may take a lot of excavating before you understand why you are disinclined to deal with the marketplace. I hope that you can do that excavating, because avoiding the marketplace usually leads to shutting down your creative impulses and avoiding creating altogether. If, when you do that excavating, you can't quite figure out what is going on inside of you, you can make the following pledge and follow through on it: "I may not know *why* I'm avoiding the marketplace, but that avoidance must end! Okay, marketplace, here I come!"

# Chapter 11

## PICKING, PROTECTING, AND HONORING YOUR CREATIVE SPACE

It's harder to unleash your creative potential if your physical environment works against you. Yes, you can block out that jackhammering. Yes, you can work with all those bills piled up and in your face. Yes, you can work scrunched up in your jam-packed storeroom. But are those difficulties likely deterring you and even thwarting you? Quite possibly.

The physical realities of your work space matter. What matters even more is how you treat that space. Do you protect it? Do you honor it? Let's look at the issues of picking, protecting, and honoring your creative space from the perspective of a writer who is endeavoring to write. Please translate this advice so that it makes sense for your creative discipline: for your painting studio, your home recording studio, your dance space, your ceramic studio. Each space will have its own particular requirements, but this applies to each: **your space needs to be chosen, protected, and honored.**

Often enough the places that are available to us in which to write do not suit us simply because we are not inclined to write. It may be a matter of everyday resistance; it may be that meaning has vanished; it may be that we can't tolerate the creative process; it may be any one of the issues we've been discussing.

One client, an American poet living in Amsterdam with his Dutch wife and their two daughters, could not write in his perfectly fine study because the silence was slightly off, his chair was slightly ill-fitting, his desk was slightly at the wrong height, and his door, which didn't lock, was often open. The very threat of that door opening stopped him from writing. He knew that he was being "neurotic" about all this, but he nevertheless clung to his certainty that his space was not conducive to writing. So he didn't write. Of course, his physical space wasn't the issue. But it somehow served him to imagine that it was.

Sometimes something about your physical space is, indeed, an issue—not *the* issue but *an* issue. Take the following example. A client of mine took one large step after another in order to position herself to write her first book. She gave up her lucrative, sixty-hour-a-week day job. She convinced her husband that they should move to a rural area where the quiet would be conducive to thinking and writing. They moved to a rugged, beautiful spot, purchased a house with stunning views, and reinvented themselves—he as a consultant; she as an online content writer for websites. They loved their new life; they loved the fact that deer visited and that storms whipped through the valley. But she couldn't begin her book.

Every morning she came into her study, with its stupendous views through floor-to-ceiling windows, and felt a kind of paralysis. So as to be doing something, she'd check her e-mail, attend to business, and keep busy hour after hour until it was time to take a walk in the woods or have lunch with her husband. The morning would pass this way, efficiently enough, productively enough, and sadly. The afternoon would prove even harder—more everyday work accomplished, more sadness, more hours spent not writing her book.

She could perfectly attribute her paralysis: her parents had criticized her. She didn't feel confident. She hadn't written a book before. She wasn't certain what the book was supposed to be about. She found her writing workmanlike, not sizzling. Her husband was a little needy and distracted her with his presence. She had to do her online writing to make money. Part of her found her book not important enough to write. Another part of her found her book not interesting enough to write. She got headaches easily. She'd never gotten her two short stories published, which was demoralizing. People loved her writing, but their praise seemed unearned and so she dismissed it and even turned it into criticism. Her paralysis made perfect sense to her.

I told her I understood. I told her she was making one critical "mental mistake": thinking that she was writing a book. The word *book* appeared to have the iconic, mesmerizing power to snuff out the possibility of writing. She was inadvertently picturing her book among other books like *War and Peace* and *Crime and Punishment*, books that overwhelmed her and made her feel small and incapable. I told her it was a big mistake to think she was writing a book. In fact, what she was writing was a draft. The book would come later—perhaps much later—after countless pratfalls. She had no book to write, only a draft.

She agreed that my observation made sense and she knew what she needed to do: the work. And, indeed, she tried. But the startling vista that confronted her in her study, a vista so large and engaging that even if you turned your back on it you felt its presence and its immensity, hurt rather than helped her. The floor-to-ceiling windows, devoid of covering, let in too much distraction. She tried moving her chair, turning her desk, averting her eyes, but nothing worked. Finally, she decided to poke about the house and look for another workspace. She came upon a small windowless room, not much larger than a walk-in closet, stepped inside it, and felt right silence descend instantly. This became her writing space. Finally, she began her novel.

Once you internally agree to get your work done, you can write almost anywhere. But that doesn't mean you can vanish into your writing as easily in one environment as in another. In our first small house, I had a windowless basement study that was perfect for me. In our next house, a big suburban one, I had a score of objectively excellent writing spots and none of them felt congenial. In the upscale city apartment that followed, we had panoramic views that proved paralyzing. In our next small Edwardian flat, a room at either end suited me splendidly: the room at the eastern end bright in the morning, the room at the western end bright in the afternoon.

Which spot in your house will be your primary creative space? Get up and start your investigations. Give every reasonable spot a try and every unreasonable spot too. Some writing spots are more congenial than others. Find your best one or create it, if it doesn't exist, by pushing furniture around, reclaiming the storeroom, ventilating the attic, doing whatever is necessary. If you're a painter, a singer, a musician, or other creative, you can and should follow these same steps.

Next is the matter of protecting that space and your creative life. Your husband comes home from work. You talk with him, have a drink together, have dinner. Then you go to your creative space, close the door, boot up your computer, empty your mind, and ready yourself to continue your novel.

Right about the time the desktop icons appear on your computer screen, your husband storms into your study to complain about the automobile insurance premiums. Don't you agree that it's time to switch to another company? Out of politeness, you listen to him vent about the price of insurance, the price of gas, and the price of his favorite cereal. You've heard this rant so often, you can repeat it word for word. You grit your teeth and wait for the rant to end.

When he's finally done, you turn to your computer screen and discover that you are entirely in the wrong frame of mind to write. You are angry with your husband, angry with yourself, frustrated about how long it's taking you to write this novel, and suddenly exhausted. You turn off the computer and go to bed.

You didn't protect your writing life very well, did you?

It's six thirty in the morning. You're at your computer, half-ready to write, but you decide to check your e-mail one more time (you checked it already first thing, five minutes previously). A mildly interesting, mildly important e-mail has arrived about an event benefiting a cause you support. You could wait to deal with it, but you decide to deal with it right away.

You craft your reply, which takes twenty minutes. You decide to whom you want to forward the message, then realize that you had better send a little explanation along with the e-mail. That takes another hour. Now you're hungry; and more e-mails have come in; and you planned only to write from six thirty till eight, because you have many other things to do. So you make a date with yourself to write at 4:00 p.m. You answer a few new e-mails, get up from the computer at nine, and compliment yourself on three productive hours at your desk.

You didn't protect your writing life very well, did you?

The power company is digging up the street in front of your house, which is where your study is located. You sit there in front of your computer and can't write a word because heavy machinery rumbles up and down the street and men with jackhammers crack through the pavement. You feel proud that you aren't running out of the room, screaming, but you can't get a lick of work done.

Of course, you could move to the back of the house, where it is relatively quiet, which would take you about a minute to do, because your computer is a laptop and completely portable. It even has a charged battery. But, so you say, you don't write in the back of the house; you only write in your study. So you sit there, fuming; your head throbbing; and after another few agonizing minutes you throw in the towel and shut down your computer.

You didn't protect your writing life very well, did you?

Your in-laws are visiting. You could go to your study, or you could sit with them over breakfast. You've already had nine consecutive meals with them, and there isn't a thing left to chat about, except perhaps the things you disagree about. Nevertheless, you  choose to sit with them. You make them their dry toast and put out the orange marmalade and mutter, "I thought I might get a little writing done this morning." Your mother-in-law exclaims, "By all means!" which you take to mean that she's as sick of you as you are of her. But you hear yourself say, "Oh no, that's okay. I'll join you for breakfast." You bring your slice of toast to the table, and the small talk begins.

You didn't protect your writing life very well, did you?

Your days are full, and you only have two hours in the evening in which to write. Your teenage daughter, whom you love, is learning Italian and wants to practice with you. You don't mind this because you have your heart set on a trip to Italy and want to know how to do more than order espresso and find the bathroom. So you practice Italian with her.

This is pleasant and even a blessing, to be spending time with her. But no writing gets done. You'd like to stop the practicing, but you don't know how to get out of it without disappointing your daughter. So you keep practicing. One day you discover that you can order a complete meal in Italian, but your novel is no closer to being finished.

You didn't protect your writing life very well, did you?

What should you have done?

Scenario 1: Locked the door. Or said to your husband, "Dear, I'm working. But I'll be happy to discuss the insurance in about an hour."

Scenario 2: Skipped dealing with that "important" e-mail, which you could have dealt with in the evening.

Scenario 3: Moved to the back of the house, even though you "don't write there."

Scenario 4: Let them eat breakfast while you got a little writing done.

Scenario 5: Said to your daughter, "This has been ever so pleasant! Now I need to get back to my novel."

You are the only one who can protect your creative space and creative life. To protect them, you may have to enlist the aid of your family. You may have to let your husband know when the insurance discussions will occur, inform your children that you are completely available to them except for those two hours each evening when you are utterly unavailable, and explain to your in-laws that their visit is an amazing gift but that you also intend to get some creating done.

If you're a painter with a studio in a painting cooperative where painters wander in and out to socialize, it may mean locking the door to the studio while you're working. If you're a fabric artist, it may mean reclaiming the workroom that's become the all-purpose storage room. You may have to protect your creative space with soundproofing and with Do Not Enter signs. Your creative space is a literal space, and it's also a metaphoric space. Both need protection: the first with explicit rules; the second with strong intentions.

Some things to do? Write out a security pledge: how you will protect your creative space and creative life. Have a discussion with anyone who currently invades your creative space and spell out your new ground rules. Protect your creative space with a talisman, amulet, or icon. Then write a little, safe and snug in your protected space.

It likewise matters what you do when you are in your creative space. It matters whether you are working on your novel or surfing the Internet. It matters whether you are pining for the one agent who will fall in love with your writing or preparing to query thirty agents. It matters whether you are building your platform by offering to write columns, speak at churches, and lead teleseminars or whether you are fantasizing about who will play the lead when your novel is made into a movie. Sitting in your space isn't enough; it matters what you do there.

It matters whether you are writing your second novel, even though your first one hasn't sold yet, or brooding that you aren't published. It matters whether you are writing an e-mail to your literary agent, with whom you haven't been in contact for six months, or waiting for the phone to ring with news that she's sold your novel. It matters whether you are honorably revising your novel, for the fifth time, because it's still muddled in spots, or doing everything you can to avoid its muddles. It matters what you are doing.

It matters whether you are contemplating some shortcut—maybe stealing a few scenes from that first novel that went awry and dropping them into your current novel, where they might possibly fit—or sitting up straight in your chair and writing the scenes your novel needs. It matters whether you are thinking of hiring an editor, a ghostwriter, or even the handyman to write your book, because you are completely sick of it and can't face it, or whether you are biting the bullet, brewing tea, and hunkering down to write.

It matters whether you are sitting in the dark with the shades drawn and your computer off, because you are sad and depressed, or whether you are helping yourself out of your depression by whatever means possible. If that means getting out of the house, that's what it means. Better that than sitting in your creative space inert and morose.

Honoring your creative space means that if you are embroiled in tasks, dramas, crises, and errands, you ring a bell at your appointed time and let all of that go. You enter your creative space clear and unencumbered. If you are tired from your day job, you splash water on your face. If you are exhausted from your mate's chatting, you take an aspirin and a quick nap. If you have a hundred things to do before you get to write, you put aside that long list and remind yourself what honor means.

Honoring your creative space means that if you need to read what you've previously written, you read it. If you need to plunge forward without rereading, you plunge forward. You accept that you have craft to master, attention to pay, and a routine to follow. You refuse to attribute any of your shortcomings to your "artistic nature." You get off your high horse, sit right down on your swivel chair, do the work, and honor the process.

At the same time, you set the bar sufficiently high. It is fine to write articles, but is it fine to never write your book? It is fine to begin your thirtieth journal, but is it fine to have written only journal entries and not your book? It may seem funny to get off your high horse and set the bar high, but the two go together beautifully. You agree to work without fanfare, and you choose work equal to your dreams.

You honor your creative space by recovering, if you are an addict. You honor your creative space by becoming an anxiety expert, a real pro at mindfulness and personal calming. You honor your creative space by affirming that you matter, that your writing life matters, and that your current writing project matters. You honor your creative space by entering it with this mantra: "I am ready to work." You enter, grow quiet, and vanish into your writing.

*Honor* is a funny word, a loaded word, a difficult word. It is not a word to toss around lightly. But I'm willing to bet that you place it at the very top of your list of words with personal meaning. I bet you love it, believe in it, and aspire to it. Live that way then! Honor the fact that you believe in honor, and construct your writing life around it.

If you live your life as you intend it to be lived, you will find yourself in your creative space thousands of times. Sixty years of writing, two hours a day, translates to better than fifty thousand hours in your creative space. Squander a number of those hours; we all must. Be in a bad mood for a few of those hours, just like everyone else. Write poorly during some of those hours; there's no way around that. But try your best to honor your creative space. That's the key intention.

When I train creativity coaches, I ask them to do the following. I ask them to make a list of the things that they will never do in their creative space and to keep that list handy, right beside their computer. I ask them to make a list of the things that they will only occasionally do in their creative space and to keep that list handy, right beside their computer. And I ask them to make a list of the things that they intend to do most of the time they are in their creative space and to keep that list handy, right beside their computer. Here are two responses to this exercise.

Maria explained: "This week I committed to protecting my creative space. I am breaking through a lifetime of messages on practicality and about making a living from my writing, and making a commitment to protect my creative space is huge for me. It feels great, although I don't yet trust my follow-through, which feels very fragile. But I truly feel that my writing life has seriously begun by taking this simple step.

"I am protecting my creative space and my writing time by putting three weekly sessions of thirty minutes each into my electronic calendar. I've set two electronic reminders for each session to automatically pop up. I took the time to think very carefully about where in my week to put these sessions, so to set myself up to win. I committed to three small sessions because I want to get some 'showing up' success under my feet before I add more writing time.

"My actual creative place needs no protection, only from myself! I decided that going upstairs rather than writing in bed or in the living room will work best for me, to help me focus and to ritualize the writing. I will light a candle and set a timer. If I need or want to spend more writing time there, I can. Sometimes I will play Native American flute music or another instrumental music in the background softly, to help me feel calm.

"My husband is very respectful of my space, so he's not as much of a problem as I am. I'm often engaging him and connecting with him that he could use the break from me! He would love to see me move forward and take this time to develop my writing. So for now it's timers, candles, soft instrumentals, calendars, and reminders that will best help me solidify this practice and habit."

Laura explained: "Writing about my procrastination last week was a wake-up call. It finally got me to admit to myself how bad my 'not creating' had gotten. I think this is partly to do with my struggle to find a voice for my blog, a voice that feels like it's my own, after years of writing to the house style of various newspapers and magazines.

"I had not been honoring my creative space at all. Here's what I've done to protect it.

"1. Had a boundary-setting conversation with my family. We agreed that when my study door is shut, it means I'm working and it should be opened only if whatever they have to say is urgent, important, and really, really can't wait.

"2. I do a lot of other things at my desk, other than writing. It's where I sit to coach clients. It's where I do the accounts and administration for a property side-business I run with my partner. It's where I pay bills, study, and research. It's also where I waste a lot of time watching TED talks, playing daft online games, answering unnecessary e-mails, and reading news/social media sites. I will stop this.

"3. From now on, when I am writing, I have decided to light a candle and set it on my desk, as a reminder that I am there to write and do nothing else. When the candle is lit, I will quit my browser, and if that doesn't stop me, I'll get one of those Internet-blocking apps and set it for the length of time I've decided to write.

"4. I will check e-mail briefly first thing, in case there is something urgent. If there isn't (which is most of the time),

I won't deal with e-mails, admin, or anything else until after I've done my writing. If there is something that needs dealing with urgently, I'll deal with it. But only that. Games, TED talks, and all the other distractions can't happen at all until I've done my day's work. And even then, if they can be done on my iPad in a different room, that's where I'll do it.

"5. If, for any reason, I'm finding it hard to work at home, I will go to a nearby coffee shop. (For some reason if I'm in a distracted mood, the background babble of a coffee shop seems to help me focus. Plus, there's caffeine.) I've followed this all week and gotten one or two hours of concentrated writing in every day, which feels like a minor miracle. I've roughed out a thirty-day e-mail course that I can offer for free as an incentive to sign up to my mailing list. Next week I'm in England for most of the week, but I'm committing, here and now, to somehow continue this routine while there, to writing the whole course and getting it up and running in a couple of weeks."

It is our work to pick, protect, and honor our creative space, and it is our work to protect our creative life—often from ourselves. This week try the exercise of listing what you will never do in your creative space, what you will do only occasionally there, and what you will do most or all of the time there. See what you learn!

# Chapter 12

## SPEAKING UP AND ASKING FOR WHAT YOU NEED

Most people find it hard to speak up. What does this difficulty look like in the life of a creative or a would-be creative? A painter came to see me. She explained that her husband, who had recently retired, kept visiting her in her studio space to chat about inconsequential matters. I asked her to craft a sentence of seven words or fewer that communicated what she wanted to say to him about the preciousness of her painting time and space.

Her first efforts were long and apologetic. Finally, after many tries, she arrived at: "I can't talk while I'm working."

"Can you say that to him?" I asked.

"Yes," she replied.

"How does that feel?" I continued.

"Very, very scary."

Next, we role-played a situation she was having with the fellow who did printing work for her. He was the only person in her area equipped to do this printing work, and she liked both the work he did and his prices. But he was always inappropriate with her, saying things like, "You know, I have feelings for you" and "Most husbands don't understand their artist wives."

"What do you want to say to him?" I asked. Having just practiced, she was quicker to respond. "I need you to stop that," she said. "I am coming here to have prints made, period." She laughed. "That's two sentences, and one's a little long. But that's the idea, right?"

"That's exactly the idea," I agreed.

You help manifest your creative potential by saying strong, clear things. Saying them in seven words or fewer is a great practice. Here are examples of responses of seven words or fewer that people are unlikely to make unless they have done a bit of practicing beforehand. The phrases I have in mind are in bold.

- Someone drops you an e-mail saying that she loves your work, though she can't afford to buy any of it. Typically, you might reply with a "Thank you" and leave it at that. The new, bolder you might reply, "Thank you.

**Might you tell your friends about me?** I'd appreciate that!"

■ You're at a party, you find yourself chatting with someone about your art, and you have your usual difficult time explaining what it is you paint. The effort to explain yourself exhausts you, and you have the sense that you haven't done a very good job of it. In such situations, it isn't likely that you're going to find a bold note to end on. However, because you've practiced, you indeed manage a bold note and say, **"Would you like to visit my studio?"** Rather than presuming that you've made a hash of your explanations, you propose a visit.

■ Your sister asks you if you can take over minding your aging mother because "you don't have a real job." You could meekly agree and lose several years of your life, or you could say, **"My painting is real work."** Then you might continue, "Let's work out something equitable among all us kids, because we all have jobs and lives."

■ You meet someone who says that her blog for new mothers is very popular. You might reply,

"Great!" or you might reply, "Great! **Might your peeps be interested in me**?" Probably she is going to reply, "Gee, I don't know. Offhand I wouldn't think so," to which you might reply, "Yes, I understand, but let me tell you why they might."

- You get an e-mail from an artist you know announcing his participation in a group show. You could congratulate him, or you could congratulate him and ask, **"Room for one more in the show?"**

- You read a blog post in an online magazine about something tangentially related to the subject matter you paint. You could nod to yourself and move on, or you could drop the blogger a quick e-mail and say, "Loved your post on firehouses! My art is right up that alley! **Care to do a piece on me?**"

Is there something you really ought to be saying to your husband or wife? To your mother or father? To one of your children? To someone at your day job? To your business manager, your literary agent, your gallery owner, your editor, your director, your conductor, your band members?

A first step may be speaking the words in an empty room. Just saying them out loud may prove empowering. Once you've said them, you can hear how they really sound. Did they sound much less dangerous than you supposed they would? Even almost innocuous? If so, that knowledge may help you feel safer and make it more likely that you will say those words "for real" to the person in question.

In answer to the question "Where am I obliged to speak up?" you may discover that there are many places where it is necessary. Don't let that fact overwhelm or discourage you. Pick one place to speak and begin there. If this is feeling very risky and scary, pick what feels like the easiest or safest place to speak. Speak there, and use that as a stepping-stone to your next act of courageous speaking.

We had better speak up because self-censorship is a great silencer and inhibitor. Freud suspected that all cases of writer's block were instances of self-censorship. It wasn't that the writer didn't have words or ideas but that for some reason they were afraid to express them and to share them. Self-censorship is a huge issue for all human beings, creatives most definitely included.

Think of how difficult this is for a research scientist contemplating presenting a controversial theory, a painter contemplating a suite of antisocial paintings, or a novelist contemplating writing a novel whose theme is revenge. What are we afraid that we might reveal? That we aren't as smart as we'd like to think we are. That we aren't as talented. That we aren't as accomplished. That our performance leaves a lot to be desired. That our writing is uninspired. That our visual imagery is trite. That we're second-rate. That we're derivative. That we're disgusting. That we're behind the times. That we're childish. . . .

Plus, it can feel frankly unsafe to say what's on our mind. To make a political or social statement in a blog post, an essay, a book, a song, or a painting is to invite pushback; criticism; ruptures; retaliation; financial, familial, and job consequences; and even imprisonment or death. It is completely reasonable to take seriously the consequences of speaking our mind. But taking those consequences seriously and deciding never to speak are two different things. The first is prudence; the second is abject silence.

What can help? A dedicated speaker's corner in the room that is your mind. Historically, the most famous speaker's corner was the northeast corner of Hyde Park in London. But there are other speaker's corners, both in England and around the world. There are speaker's corners in Indonesia, the Netherlands, Italy, Canada, Australia, Singapore, Thailand, and elsewhere. They provide a designated "safe place" for a person to speak his or her mind—though, contrary to popular belief, not all speech is permitted there. In the speaker's corner that you create in your mind, *all* speech is permitted.

Why might you be censoring yourself? You might be a Darwin and worried about how your naturalistic views will be received in an intolerant religious environment. You might be a Goya and worried about how your activist paintings will be received in a repressive, authoritarian environment. You might be a James Baldwin and worried about how your homoerotic writings will be received in a virulently homophobic environment. Whatever the sources of your self-censorship happen to be, you don't want to censor yourself before you've had a chance to speak your mind—at least to yourself. Use your speaker's corner to practice speaking all things dangerous and unmentionable.

How might you use your speaker's corner? Say that you've been writing a novel and you've gotten stuck and blocked. This may have happened for any number of reasons, but one may be self-censorship. Go to your speaker's corner. Speak your novel's darkest, most difficult truths. See how they sound out loud. Are they not so dangerous as to be excluded? Or do they reveal too much about you and really must be avoided? Do your brave speaking, engage in your equally brave evaluating, and see what you've learned.

Maybe you'll be able to immediately resume writing your novel. Maybe you'll have learned how to revise it strategically. Maybe you'll understand why it must be abandoned. The chances are excellent that your courageous efforts will have produced useful movement. A surprisingly hard challenge for creatives is counteracting self-censorship and courageously speaking. Creating a speaker's corner in your mind and using it to speak up can help end that self-censorship.

A variation on the theme of "speaking up" is "asking for what you want and need." We discuss these matters in the creativity coaching trainings I facilitate. Joanna, a coach-in-training, explained:

"On the subject of not feeling up to asking, I think I recently made the following realization and it has changed a lot for me. 'Not feeling up to asking' is about being able to receive. I always felt that I had to have lots of money to afford help. This year I asked for help in various areas. Some I paid, a few I did exchanges, and others I just said thank you.

"For my recent art exhibition in Paris, I posted on Facebook: 'Who wants to help me set up?' and I had an artist whom I hardly knew come. It took us three hours to set up, instead of a whole day by myself, and we spent two hours in a café after. It was the first time I did that. Before, I always did everything by myself because I didn't want to bother anybody.

"I did the same asking when it came time to take down the exhibit and another artist I hardly knew traveled three hours to come and help me! Since I changed my mind-set, I see so many people who can help me. They were there all along!

"I now pay my daughter to create my marketing visuals, my thirteen-year-old tech-wiz nephew to edit my videos, and a marketing friend to write my press releases, media kit, retreat announcements, and conference write-ups. A young woman approached me to help set up and sell a training course for businesses, and I will pay her with a percentage on the gigs she finds.

"All of this has been transformational for me. After twelve years of working really hard on my art career, trying to learn the trades needed, I don't feel overwhelmed with all the tasks anymore. And it's far more fun to work with others! I've helped people and volunteered countless times in my life. It's time I experienced being on the receiving side!"

Let's take a look at how "speaking up" and "asking for what you want and need" might come together in the hypothetical example of a singer/songwriter who is in the process of making her own CD and paying for it out of her own pocket.

Our singer/songwriter, Jane, has hired a well-known and very busy freelance producer, Jack, to work with her. This process of making a CD is almost always fraught with plenty of difficulties, because Jane has to get studio time scheduled far in advance, she is tied to Jack's availability, and Jack is expensive. Therefore, it is vitally important that she speak up and ask for what she wants and needs if she is to have a successful experience.

Let's frame this hypothetical example in terms of ten tips:

1. **When you want someone to understand you, be clear.** Jane could say to Jack, "Can we get together sometime in mid–March and work on the album a little?" but that doesn't really communicate enough to Jack about her needs or about his reality. It would be much better if Jane said something like "I can book studio time on March 7, March 8, or March 9 at the following hours. Does one of those times work for you? If not, can you give me times that will work? But I do hope one of these times works, because the studio is booked up and it's going to

be hard to find other dates. So if you can make it on March 7, 8, or 9, that would be great!"

2.  **When you want someone to understand you, be brief.** It is wise to understand that people are not helped when they are bombarded by a ton of information. For example, Jane could write Jack a long e-mail about all the reasons why she is having trouble getting her last few songs written or she could say, "Ten songs are done, and the last two aren't. How do you think we should proceed?" Not only is this more helpful, but explaining herself briefly and clearly will actually clarify matters to Jane herself.

3.  **When you want someone on your side, be affirmative.** It is not brilliant to think that people don't notice when they are criticized or that they won't get defensive. Jane could say to Jack, "I don't think you are hearing me when I say that I need the drums to be less assertive," which is a criticism. On the other hand, she could say, "I'm loving our process together! I only wonder if I'm being clear enough about the drums? I'd love it if they

could be muted a little. Do you think that would be okay?" You try the honey approach until you are forced to turn to vinegar. Don't lead with vinegar.

4. **Make sure that you've been heard by checking in and by asking questions.** Often checking in isn't enough. You need to make sure you've been heard and understood. Jane might write to Jack and say, "Did you get the long e-mail I sent you the other day?" Or she might write and say the more effective "In that e-mail I sent you the other day, I fear I might not have been clear on a couple of points, specifically on the timing of our next recording sessions and on your hourly rate going up in June. Were my thoughts on those two matters clear?"

5. **Don't let your nerves stop you from delivering your message.** Jane may have something very important that she needs to get clear with Jack, but dealing with him may be making her anxious. It isn't going to benefit her to let her nerves get the better of her since he is producing her album. Her best bet is to recognize that dealing with him makes

her anxious, accept that reality, make use of anxiety management strategies, bite the bullet, and talk to him. When people matter to us the way the producer of our album matters to us, we mustn't let anxiety keep us from communicating with them.

6. **When warning bells go off, hold your tongue—at least long enough to gather your thoughts.** Let's say that Jack says to Jane, "Oh, I'll be bringing my fees up to market rate in June." Jane would want to think about her reply rather than blurt out, "But we agreed to work through the end of this album at your current rate!" or "I'm not going to be able to handle a higher rate. This is a disaster!" By holding her tongue and taking time to gather her thoughts, she will do a better job of not only saying what serves her but intuiting where Jack is coming from and empathizing with him. Having done that careful work, she can send Jack an e-mail that is affirmative, brief, and clear that either asks for clarification or that spells out her arguments for his continuing to work at his current rates.

7. **Never treat marketplace communications cavalierly.** If you are Jane and during a recording session you're disappointed with the way the bass player played, you don't want to blurt out to Jack, "We need a new bass player!" Certainly not if you are just beginning to think the matter through and haven't decided whether you do or don't want a new bass player. If you bring the matter up before you really mean to, you've made internal work for Jack, who now has to worry about the whole bass player question. If you don't want Jack to begin thinking about something, don't say it.

8. **Respond to marketplace messages in a calculated way.** Let's say Jack mentions to Jane that he is getting married. Jane can congratulate him and think nothing more of it, or she can reckon that with a marriage comes a honeymoon and he is going to be less available in June than he otherwise might have been. Therefore, Jane can congratulate him *and* say the following, which is calculated to help herself: "Wow, Jack, that means May and June are going to be awfully busy for you! I wonder if we

should book extra hours in April to make sure the project gets done."

9. **Get brilliant about hidden agendas.** Let's say Jack tells Jane about a song he previously liked: "This song about horses isn't quite there yet. I wonder if you want to take time and get it ready before we go into the studio again." If Jane takes this message at face value, it will sound like criticism and may affect her relationship with Jack and even make her doubt the song and her album. But if she is smart about human nature and the extent to which people carry hidden agendas, it may occur to her that perhaps something else is going on. So she might reply, "That's an idea. But I wonder if something is up in your life and you need time away from my project? Is that why you're wanting me to take another look at the horse song?" She may have guessed right, or she may have guessed wrong. But by checking in with Jack in this way, she has a shot at unearthing his hidden agendas, if there are any, while at the same time not getting down on the song or herself.

10. **If you can't decode an important communication, ask for clarification.** Let's say Jack tells Jane, "You know, I was working on Sarah's album yesterday, and I'm really falling in love with the way she holds her notes over the fade-outs." Jane may suspect that this is a message intended for her, but unless she asks for clarification she won't know. If she doesn't ask, she'll brood about whether Jack was saying something to her or not saying something to her. Her best bet is to frankly ask, "Is what Sarah's doing applicable to my album, or were you just saying something nice about Sarah?" Whatever Jack's answer, it is bound to clarify what he was intending by his remark.

Creating, by its very nature, is a form of "speaking up." And it follows that if you are having trouble speaking up, you will have trouble creating. You will likewise have trouble creating if you can't ask for what you need: for instance, that your partner stop disparaging you, that your literary agent communicate more often with you, or that your parents stop going on about when you will get a real job. It takes courage to speak up and ask for what you want and need. Be brave and do just that!

# Conclusion

## COMPLETING CREATIVE PROJECTS

It is hard to get our creative work done, but it is extra hard to get it completed. Certain difficulties and resistances arise as we near the end of projects. This is regularly the case and causes many creatives and would-be creatives untold pain that it will pay us to patiently examine these extra special difficulties. Why is finishing a novel, a memoir, a song, or a painting problematic for artists? Here are twelve reasons, framed from the point of view of a painter.

**1. The painting-in-progress doesn't match your original vision for the piece.** Very often an artist "sees" her painting before it is painted—in all its beauty, grandeur, and excellence—and then as she paints, the "real" painting doesn't match the brilliance and perfection of the original vision. Disappointed, she loses motivation to complete her creative project and either white-knuckles her way to the end or doesn't complete it.

One solution? Understand that your real paintings will be different from your imagined paintings. The reality of process pretty much guarantees that the work you are doing will "go its own way" and will become the thing it will become, not a remembered or idealized version of itself. Maturely accept that any feelings you may harbor for the remembered or idealized should not prevent you from accepting and appreciating the real one in front of you.

**2. The hard bits won't come.** Even if you successfully complete 99 percent of your art, if 1 percent remains that isn't working or doesn't satisfy you, then that work of art remains incomplete in your own estimation.

What do artists try to do in this situation?

- Some have the happy experience of returning to that 1 percent, and the solution suddenly presents itself.

- Some decide to "keep fussing with" the troubled area, finally bringing it to completion or making a mess of the whole thing.

- Some decide to call the work of art "finished for now" and put it out in the world with that nagging 1 percent still lacking.

- Some decide to step away from the work for a period of time, either in the hope that when they come back to it they will know what to do or the problem will have vanished of its own accord.

- Some abandon the work altogether and number it among those creative efforts that didn't quite pan out.

There is no perfect solution to this natural dilemma. It is simply the case that sometimes a part of the thing we are working on isn't coming around. Because this is true so often, many of our creative efforts are held hostage to this problem. Stop for a moment and see if you can come up with answers to this question: "When 1 percent remains recalcitrant and intractable, what tactics will I employ to get to the end?"

**3. The fear that this is your best idea.** Let's say you've been working for months on a large, complicated narrative painting. You've figured out how to take a mythological subject and put it into modern dress, and you're proud of and excited by your idea.

Naturally enough, your brain has organized itself around this idea, is focused on this painting, and isn't allowing neurons to fly off and think about other paintings. This natural phenomenon of being focused has a shadow side: it can make you believe you don't currently have another good idea and that you *won't* have another good idea . . . ever. You can get weighed down by the feeling that since no other idea will ever come to you, you had better nurse this one— so as to have something to work on and to put off what you feel will be a terrible moment of reckoning when, with this painting done, you face the void and discover you have nothing left to say.

The antidote is simply to say "No!" to this half-conscious thought. Even if no next idea is currently present, that is no reason to presume an excellent idea won't percolate up when the time is right, after this painting is completed.

**4. The appraising will have to begin.** While you're working on a piece, you can keep saying to yourself, "Yes, it isn't wonderful yet, but by the end it will be!" You hold out the carrot that your further efforts will transform the work into something you really love. But once you say it is complete, then you actually have to appraise it and decide if it is even any good.

Because we likely want to put off that moment of reckoning, we are inclined to say, "Well, let me do just a little more." Out of conscious awareness, we may know that there isn't really anything more to do and that doing more will actually harm the work. But we continue to tinker because we don't want to have to confront the question, "Okay, since I am calling it done, is it any good?"

The answer: accept that appraising is coming and it isn't the end of the world. You may be wonderfully and pleasantly surprised, or you may be disappointed and demoralized. Whatever the outcome, it isn't the end of the world. You can chalk your effort up to process, part of your apprenticeship, and the natural fact that only a percentage of our work will prove to be excellent. Move right on. Try not to continue working on a project because you fear the moment of appraisal.

**5. Lack of a "completion checklist."** If you're building a house and approaching the end of the project, you create a punch list of things that have to get done: spot painting, putting in a switch plate or light fixture, etc. When you've completed everything on your list, you can be certain you are finished. Yes, you have to look around to see if you've missed anything. But you can feel confident that because you got everything checked off, you are really done.

By contrast, visual artists have no such checklist or punch list, would never dream of creating one, and even if the concept popped into their head, would have no idea what to put on such a list. Yet it can prove helpful to consider this checklist idea and see if it might serve you.

**6. Lingering doubts.** It's very hard for people not to doubt themselves sometimes—especially when it comes time to saying that one of their creative projects is successfully completed. Artists who finish a painting may almost instantly have their mind throw up a doubt or other unhelpful thought:

- "Maybe I should do more because there's always more to do."

- "Maybe I'm done, but am I really 100 percent certain about that cast shadow over there on the right?"

- "Maybe I'm done, but it doesn't exactly look like what I had in mind."

- "Maybe I'm done, but have I really answered all those objections raised by the gallery owner in London about whether I'm successfully cultivating a unique painting style?"

- "Maybe I'm done, but . . . "

If one of these is the habitual way your mind plays tricks on you and keeps you from completing things in a timely appropriate way, it is your job to get a grip on your mind. When you hear yourself doubting yourself in one of these unfortunate ways, exclaim, "No! I know that thought! It doesn't serve me and I don't want it! No, you darn thought.

No!" Only you are in the position to put doubts of these sorts to rest.

**7. Ongoing conflicts about what and how much to reveal.** All artists expose themselves in their art. One artist may expose her sexual fantasies or obsessions. Another artist may expose his rages and resentments. A third may expose an unpopular belief or violate a cultural rule or norm. An abstract artist may fear that her audience will suppose that she can't really draw, even though she can. Even the most "innocent" or unobjectionable sort of work, where, for example, the subject matter is a bowl of apples or a vase of roses, is an exposure of sorts, perhaps in a conflicted artist's mind exposing her lack of innovation or imagination.

All art says something about the artists—and artists may be conflicted about whether they like what their art says about them or what it reveals. The easiest way to deal with this conflict is to not complete things. Then no one will ever see your art, and no ridicule or humiliation is possible. Many artists fail to complete their works because they are in an inner battle about whether or not they are happy about what their art reveals about them.

The answer is to bring this conflict into conscious awareness and deal with it. Decide one way or the other whether you are willing to reveal your sexual fantasies, your simmering rage, or your disagreements with society. Say out loud, "I am not worried in the slightest that I'll be charged with not being able to draw" or "I don't care at all what people infer about my imagination—or lack of—because I want to paint apples and roses." Decide your position on these issues and then stand behind your decision.

**8. Difficulty knowing if and when your work of art is complete.** A minimalist, Zen-influenced painting might be done after a few strokes. A narrative painting might have a cast of dozens of characters and require countless strokes. Is the former less complete than the latter because it is minimalist and so much of the canvas remains bare? No, of course not. Each must be considered complete according to its own criteria, its own aesthetics, and its own lights. But how confusing this can become! We look at our work-in-progress and simply can't tell if it really is "done" or if it "needs more work."

Many artists have the deep, visceral feeling that their work is done early on in the process and that their continued work on it actually weakens the effect. How odd! Because "completion" is necessarily a subjective, not an objective, assessment, and we may experience multiple contradictory impressions, we must ultimately "simply" make a decision, one that is more like a guess and a surrendering than a calculation or a foregone conclusion. If we do not regularly surrender in this way and announce that a given work is done, then it isn't and never will be.

**9. Fear of losing your happy place.** You're doing a series of red paintings. All that red is making you feel happy, buoyant, and joyful. You have it in your mind that you will do a blue series next. And while that makes sense to you intellectually and aesthetically, it doesn't move your heart much. All this red feels wonderful to you; the coming blue feels a little cool, verging on cold. So to keep this loving feeling alive, you decide just out of conscious awareness not to finish these red paintings. You want a little more time with them!

The mantra to remember is that more love is available after this project is finished. Maybe the blue series will, indeed, prove cooler than the red series. But the yellow series that comes after the blue series will bring back fiery passion. You may have to mourn leaving this happy place, but leave it you must for the sake of completing your works of art and for your new loves to come.

**10. Not being ready for the process to start all over again.** Some artists can't wait to finish their current work of art and begin on the next one. They feel perpetually eager to begin, see with each new canvas or unused ball of clay a new problem to solve or a new beautiful object to make, and hold completing their current work of art as the necessary stepping-stone to the next creative adventure.

At least as many artists, however, have an opposite reaction. They find starting each new work something of a trial and even a little traumatic. Because beginning is a painful process for them, they prefer to keep working on their current project, even if it is done or could readily be completed, rather than face the unpleasant reality of another blank canvas.

If you are in this second group, you will want to heal your relationship to starting. You don't want starting to feel so terrible that it prevents you from completing. Try to answer the following question and then implement your answer: "If starting is a miserable part of the process for me, what can I do to make it feel less miserable?"

**11. Not being ready to start showing and experience all that potential criticism, silence, and rejection.** While you are working on your current piece, you can reply to anyone who asks to see it, "Sorry, it's not finished yet." If they beg, you can hold your ground and repeat your message: "Sorry, it disrupts my process if I show things before they're done." But how can you refuse them once you call the work done? What reason can you possibly offer that doesn't make it clear you're balking simply because you fear a cruel remark or an indifferent response? Once you affirm that your work is done, you don't have a leg to stand on if you try to keep it hidden.

Since artists know this, they contrive a great solution: they don't finish it. They may get "very near" to the end on many paintings, but by virtue of not having completed any of them, they achieve their half-conscious goal: they can righteously announce they have nothing to show yet. In this way, they keep all possible criticism, rejection, and marketplace negativity at bay.

The better solution is to grow a thicker skin and get easier with letting your works of art out into the world. Since every work is bound to be disliked by someone, it is indeed the case that negativity is bound to come your way. Accept that truth; surrender to it; and finish your work and show it.

**12. Not being ready to start selling and experience all that potential criticism, silence, and rejection.** Some artists are natural-born salespeople and love the marketplace. Most artists are extremely reluctant salespeople and despise treating their works of art as commodities.

Not only is selling art difficult and unpalatable, the act of submitting your works of art for sale brings up the specter—and the likelihood, verging on the certainty—that you will be met regularly and far too often by silence and indifference on the one hand, and criticism and rejection on the other.

What artist wants this silence, indifference, criticism, and rejection? Many artists find such interactions so painful that they avoid them at all costs. One simple way to avoid the painful side of selling art is to not complete your works. If you are caught up in this dynamic, try to break this cycle right now.

The following are ten tips for completing your creative projects. Give them a try!

**1. Hold the intention to complete your creative projects.** You may have many complicated, half-aware reasons for wanting to leave your creative projects unfinished. One counter to all those reasons is a strong intention to finish the work you start. With each new project say, "I intend to finish this!" Naturally, some projects will deserve to be abandoned and others will prove too difficult to complete. Those hard realities, however, are not reasons to hold anything less than an abiding desire to complete what you start.

**2. Recognize that completing your creative projects is a challenge in its own right.** Even if you want to complete your creative projects, even if you are manifesting no self-sabotaging energy or negative thoughts, finishing them may remain a real challenge. Making something good isn't easy, and making something great is that much harder. If creating an excellent thing were easy, we would see many more masterworks. But completing even quite ordinary creative work is hard in its own right. Accept this reality, and counter it with effort and energy.

**3. Get clear on why you aren't completing your creative projects.** If you're in the habit of not completing your creative projects, figure out why. There may be *one* persistent reason, there may be *several* persistent reasons, or each project may be its own situation. The possible reasons are legion. It is your job to figure out what's going on and what's keeping you from finishing projects.

**4. Consider meaning and purpose as aids to completing.** Use your ability to think about meaning and life-purpose as an aid in helping you complete your creative projects. When you get clear that finishing your creative work is likely to provide you with the psychological experience of meaning and meet your life-purpose intentions, you have more reasons for completing them than just making beautiful things that sell.

**5. Create a completion checklist.** Devise a way of creating a punch list that helps you check off tasks. If, for example, you are doing something as complicated as making an independent film, you are obliged to work from such lists if you are to keep all the myriad details straight and the enterprise on schedule. Even if you are doing something ostensibly less complicated, like writing a song, you might contrive a way of creating and using a completion checklist.

**6. Practice anxiety management.** Our doubts, worries, and nerves prevent us from getting finished. Anxiety threads its way through the creative process and is most present as we try to complete our work. Learn one or several anxiety management techniques, like deep breathing, to help you reduce your experience of anxiety and stay put as you endeavor to finish your work.

**7. Practice right thinking.** Get and keep a grip on your mind. Nothing does a better job of getting in the way of your completing creative projects than the thoughts you think that don't serve you. "I'm very busy today" or "I don't have that much energy" can do a perfect job of keeping you from tackling your current creative project. Remember the simple three-step process for dealing with thoughts that don't serve you: 1) Hear what you are thinking. 2) Actively dispute any thought that isn't serving you. 3) Substitute a more useful thought. Pay attention to this every day!

**8. If you put aside a project, create a plan for returning.** You may have excellent reasons for putting aside a creative project for the time being. But even then, you will want to create a plan or schedule for getting back to it. The plan might be as simple as, "As soon as I return from China, I will get back to my novel," or it might be more elaborate and take many eventualities and contingencies into account.

**9. Get strategic help.** You're trying to finish up your documentary, but a handful of tasks stand between you and completion. Some of them are technical and require new learning; others are artistic in areas you do not know well. You might be able to gain technical expertise, but do spending time and dealing with the stress of a steep learning curve outweigh the expense of hiring someone? Part of us naturally wants to do every- thing ourselves and retain complete control, but that stance can stop us in our tracks when we face tasks we do not know how to handle.

**10. Visualize completion and success.** It pays to picture success. If you're writing a symphony, get a clear picture in mind of an orchestra playing it. If you're painting a suite of works, visualize them on the walls of an upscale gallery. If you're working on a screenplay, enjoy the prospect of a Hollywood opening night, red carpet and all.

Visualize abundance as your body of work grows. Picture both success and completion!

Most questions having to do with completing your creative project will be answered by the act of showing up. That is your go-to tactic. But some will require careful investigation and further attention. There are many reasons why completing our creative work is difficult, but those difficulties can be met. Here's to meeting them!

# About the Author

Eric Maisel, PhD is the author of more than fifty books, including *A Writer's Paris*, *The Magic of Sleep Thinking*, and *Ten Zen Seconds*, all published by Dover Publications. He is a retired California-licensed marriage and family therapist and an active creativity coach and trainer of creativity coaches. He lectures and presents worldwide and pens the blog *Rethinking Mental Health* for *Psychology Today*. Visit www.ericmaisel.com or write to the author at ericmaisel@hotmail.com.